THE MARRIAGE PUZZLE

The Marriage Puzzle

Erwin W. Lutzer

Moody Church Media
Chicago

Disclaimer: In this volume, the verbatim intelligent transcription process simplifies and enhances spoken content by eliminating redundant words, unnecessary sounds, fixing grammar errors, and clarifying meaning while preserving the author's original intent.

THE MARRIAGE PUZZLE
Copyright © 2024 by Erwin W. Lutzer
Published by Moody Church Media
Chicago, Illinois 60614
www.moodymedia.org

Cover by Bryan Butler

ISBN: 9798336652796

All rights reserved. No part of this publication may be reproduced, stored in a retrieval system, or transmitted in any form or by any means—electronic, mechanical, digital, photocopy, recording, or any other—except for brief quotations in printed reviews, without the prior written permission of the publisher.

A transcript of the sermon series
"The Marriage Puzzle"
preached at The Moody Church, Chicago, Illinois,
between September 13 and November 15, 2009.

moodymedia.org/marriagepuzzle
Watch or listen to Pastor Lutzer's entire sermon series.

CONTENTS

Foreword 9
Red Flags You Probably Missed. 11
Moving Beyond Your Past 25
The Puzzle Of Your Roles 39
The Puzzle Of The Will Of God 51
The Puzzle Of Your Needs And Conflicts 63
The Puzzle Of Your Finances. 77
The Puzzle Of Addictions. 91
The Puzzle Of Abuse. 105
Study Guide 115

ERWIN W. LUTZER

FOREWORD

This complete transcript and study guide is intended to facilitate reflection on teaching from the Scriptures, originally preached from the pulpit of The Moody Church.

This guide is intended for both individual and group use. Included in these pages are three resources: 1.) the transcript of the messages, 2.) study guide questions with further reading and a prayer focus, and 3.) a direct link to listen to or watch the sermon series.

It might be helpful to take notes in the margins or to write in the study guide section while watching or listening to a sermon, considering how this message applies to your life. When used in a group setting, this guide will be helpful for both the group leader and participants who wish to study the passage and consider the further implications of this message.

I trust this resource will encourage and equip you in your walk with God.

Pastor Lutzer

ERWIN W. LUTZER

SERMON ONE
RED FLAGS YOU PROBABLY MISSED

Today, I begin a series of messages entitled, *The Marriage Puzzle: Why Commitment Can Do What Love Can't*. Today, we are besieged by a lot of information about marriage. We have books and seminars and sermons, and by God's grace, what I would like this series of messages to do is to be absolutely transforming. I know in order to do that, the messages aren't going to do it, only the Holy Spirit can do that. And unless you and I are open to what the Spirit of God would want to say to us, these messages might be considered to be interesting and informative but not transforming; and I aim—by the Spirit, I trust—at the transformation of marriages. By God's grace, I'd like to see bad marriages become good, and good marriages become better. For that [to happen], there's going to be a price to pay in terms of honesty in dealing with issues that have been shoved under the rug in some marriages for years.

Many marriages are like windshield wipers on a car. One does one thing, the other does another, and they never really connect. They know exactly what buttons not to push, and how they can avoid one another in the emotional and difficult thing called life. We hope to overcome that, and if you are here today and you are single, I have to emphasize to you that you need to listen because the principles we are going to be talking about will help you to understand your family—especially, should you be married someday. But in addition to that, [these are] issues all of us face, married or single. For example, the next message in this series is titled "Putting Your Past Behind You." How do you finally deal with the past in the marriage relationship or the single relationship as well?

If there's one verse of Scripture that is kind of the basis of today's message, it is found in the book of Proverbs where it says that "The fear of the LORD is the beginning of knowledge; fools despise wisdom and instruction" (Proverbs 1:7). What a verse that is, and we're going to be looking at other Proverbs in a moment. But do you understand now what I mean when I say that only the Holy Spirit can do what we want to have done—that the message can't do it? Many of you have heard many different things, and you and I know much better than we live, so who can change us? Wives can't change husbands; husbands can't change wives. Let's let God do it. Would you join me one more time in prayer? In this prayer, open your heart to what the Holy Spirit is going to tell you in the quietness of your soul.

Grant, O God, the courage for us to do whatever you show us. For those couples, Father, who are struggling, who already know in advance [the] issues they cannot address, would you break it all down and help us, and bring about marriages that honor you? In our selfishness and self-absorption, may we, as a result of these messages, deeply repent and seek only your glory in Jesus' name, Amen.

I hope you prayed that prayer.

The basis for this message grew out of an observation I made. I don't do much marriage counseling. I don't consider myself a marriage counselor, but as a pastor, I've talked to many couples and tried to help them along the bumps of their marriage. And one of the things I often ask, especially where you have people who are so mismatched or have such huge problems is: "Was there anything in your dating relationship that should have alerted you to this situation, and you should have known that this person was going to turn out this way?" Almost invariably (sometimes not, and we'll discuss that), I hear someone say something like this: "Well, yeah, in retrospect," and then they filled in the blank. And I thought to myself, "Now why aren't we wise enough to learn from those who have had this experience?" Let us look at some danger flags—red flags—that they should have picked up on and should have possibly known that they were headed for disaster. This summer at two different Bible conferences, I asked people to write me letters about their experience and the red flag they missed, or more accurately, the red flag they ignored.

So, this message is going to be a little bit different. We're going to be plunging into God's Word in a few moments, but before we do that, I'd like to just read some of these letters because we can learn from the past, and we will see that what we learn can come right out of God's Most Holy Word.

I'm going to begin with the narcissist. Narcissus, you remember, according to legend, was so enamored by his own image that as he looked into the pool and saw his reflection, he eventually drowned just looking at himself. The narcissist is the kind of person who would wear a t-shirt that says, "If you just worship me, we'll get along fine." That's the narcissist. Now, all of us are narcissists. We're all self-absorbed. I'm self-absorbed. You're self-absorbed. We're trying to move to God-absorption, but we are doing it slowly. But the true narcissist, the real genuine article, is really a piece of work, and I could tell you much about narcissists, having done some counseling and seeing them, but here's a letter:

"I thought I married Mr. Right, but I didn't know his first name was Always." [*laughter*] By the way, when you get somebody whose name is Always Right, he usually marries a woman who wants to change that first name to Never. I can already see sparks flying from here to Milwaukee. Imagine.

"During the days we dated, he never apologized for anything. If we had a disagreement or something went wrong, it was always my fault. My opinion didn't count for much. He will not discuss any viewpoint but his own. This self-absorption made me feel very lonely and rejected. We have two children who really feel disconnected from their father because he took no interest in them. All that mattered was his schedule, his work, and his friends. We can't really talk about anything that is important to both of us because he doesn't communicate. We live in the same house but we don't have a home."

How many people could testify to that? Red flag? "I saw in the dating relationship that he only cared about me for selfish reasons. Even back then, I knew he really didn't care about me as a person."

Let me read another letter, and this one is not only self-absorption, but it's also sensuality, which is a separate category.

"I got pregnant soon after we met. My husband insisted that I have an abortion, so he took me to the clinic. He showed me no sympathy or emotion. A few months after that, we were married and later we had children. A few years later, I accepted Christ as my Savior and I became convicted of the sin of aborting my baby. My husband's response was, 'Well, it's over and done. You can't do anything about it. Forget it. Move on.' This insensitivity killed my feelings for him, and in anger, to get back at him, I had an affair with his best friend. That was fifteen years ago. Today, we're committed to each other and we're working on our relationship but there are many bumps along the way."

What is the red flag? Oh, listen to this: "During our pre-marital relationship, I could see that my husband-to-be was more interested in my body than he was in me as a person. He cared about what he wanted, not about what I wanted, and he showed no sympathy toward my hurt and pain."

I have to pause here and make a couple of comments. You see, a narcissist also is not only self-absorbed. He has really no feeling for other people. He feels his own hurt very keenly, but he can't feel the hurt of other people. You take this far enough and you get a sociopath who can do evil and have no sense of conviction or guilt about it. Also, notice [she says], "My husband was more interested in my body than me as a person." Fall in love with a body, young people, and the body will deteriorate. Fall in love with a person, and the person will grow and develop and you'll have a lifetime of relationship.

I know I don't have time for all of these. We're not even going to look at all of the red flags. There are too many, and I'll be dropping those in the other messages I'm going to preach in this series, but I do need to read this one. It's the sensual person.

"I was twenty years old, a virgin, naïve with parents who were old enough to be my grandparents. They never talked to me about anything. They gave me no guidelines about whom to marry." I feel sorry for young women like that. "He was more worldly than I was, but what was I to do? I didn't know. I just assumed that that's how all men are." Listen, "I assumed his intense pursuit of me must be love." Don't ever make that assumption. Many young men pursue a young woman and they say, "I love you," and what they really mean is, "I love myself. I want you."

"Within the first months of dating, he introduced me to pornography, etc. His mother told my mother, 'Karen did well to get our son.' She thought her son was great but his father, who knew better, whispered to me, 'This is the song Kenny sings: *Me, Me, Me, I, I, I.*' Before we married, my pastor warned me and even wrote us a six-page letter, but I disregarded it. It fell on deaf ears. During our honeymoon, he brought the final draft of his thesis along and worked on it, so I was alone, especially during the day." Needless to say, after they were married she always wondered whether she was enough for him, etc. Well, they're divorced now. She says, "My ex-husband is married to a younger woman who has all the credentials of worldliness that he has. She has a ten-year-old son and she's bringing him into the marriage. The ten-year-old is struggling to have my ex-husband as his father." What a mess. "I, I, I, me, me, me."

What does the Bible say about the sensualist? "Why should you be intoxicated, my son, with a forbidden woman and embrace the bosom of an adulteress? For a man's ways are before the eyes of the LORD, and he ponders all his paths. The iniquities of the wicked ensnare him, and he is held fast by the cords of his sin."

The narcissist teaches us something. He teaches us that you should never marry unless you are willing to put the needs of someone else above your own. I forgot to read the passages of Scripture that pertain to narcissism, and for lack of time I won't, but the book of Proverbs is filled with examples of the narcissist. In fact, I'll quote it to you. Proverbs 18:2 says that the proud man is not interested in understanding. He's only interested in expressing his own opinion. There you have the narcissist, and the sensual person teaches us this: "Don't get married if you are held by the cords of sin. If you have an addiction, no matter how well hidden it is, don't marry."

Well, what was the red flag she missed? I forgot to read that also. I'm hurrying today, and I need to take my time. She said, "I knew he struggled with pornography, but I thought he'd get over it when we were married. I was wrong, wrong, wrong," she says.

What about Mr. Anger? I learned from someone that angry people can sometimes be charmers, but listen to this letter: "I married a man who was deeply angry and bitter. During our courtship he was able to hide it. He was Mr. Nice. I noticed his cynicism but thought I could live with it. There were moments when he was very charming, and very affirming."

In fact, I know of a situation where a man was so nice and doing work for other people. He was the kind of person that all the other women in the church wished they had married. And he was an abuser.

"I did not know this was a cover for some deep-seated anger and abuse. Little did I know that charmers can often be abusers. What red flag did I miss? Well, during our courtship" Listen to this. "He would sometimes hurt me and then say it was just for fun. He'd pinch me and hurt me and when I would cry out, he'd say I was just a poor sport because he was having some fun. The same was true when he would take my hand and bend it backwards until it hurt. I did not know that was the sign of an abuser. Well, now I know it was. We're divorced, though my children are walking with God."

Do I have time for one more? We need to get to the Scriptures and make sense of all of this and give people hope. By the way, the Bible is filled with verses of Scripture regarding those who are angry.

One more, number four—the lazy shirker. Here's the letter: "My husband thinks that the world owes him a living. He never held down a job and always complained about not getting paid enough. I saw all this but ignored it. He thought that life owed him. He's not an alcoholic but has all the characteristics of one. He takes no personal responsibility but continues to blame others. It's their fault he's not paid more than he is. It's their fault that they reprimand him for being late at work. It's their fault that he's not promoted. It is my fault we don't have enough money. If he loses a job, it's never his fault. It's always someone else's fault. He believes the world simply does not realize or appreciate his great abilities and contribution to the human race.

"Although we have four children, I have had to be the breadwinner and raise the children at the same time. Even though we are past middle age, my husband is still waiting around for the world to realize what a great person he really is. He applies for well-paying jobs and can't understand why he's never accepted. He thinks he deserves a high salary though he's not trained for that kind of employment. Red flag. I married the man I dated, and I saw all of this before we married but thought he'd change after we said, 'I do.' Well, he didn't change, and love is blind, so here we are."

Well, yeah, there you are. The Bible—oh, I just marvel at the book of Proverbs. Listen. I have to read these words about the lazy shirker: "As a door turns on its hinges, so does a sluggard on his bed" (Proverbs 26:14). Isn't that great? "The sluggard buries his hand in the dish and will not even bring it back to his mouth" (Proverbs 19:24). [*laughter*]. I mean that is really funny, but there are people, you know. There was a man who won a prize for being the laziest man in the world, and he was lying on a beach and somebody said, "You just won the prize of a thousand dollars for being the laziest man in the world," and he said, "Roll me over and put it in my back pocket." [*laughter*]. But here's the key: "The sluggard is wiser in his own eyes than seven men who can answer sensibly" (Proverbs 26:16). A sluggard is wiser in his own eyes. By the way, did you know the Bible connects sanity with the ability of knowing who we really are? The book of Romans says this. "I say to everyone among you not to think of himself more highly than he ought to think, but to think with sober judgment" (Romans 12:3). The Greek word is "sanely." Wow. The Bible is an absolutely overwhelming book for its accuracy.

I want to give you three characteristics of the fool. If we had taken all the passages I had outlined and read them, we'd have discovered that the fool has certain characteristics. In the book of Proverbs, you know that everything is either right or wrong. You're either a fool or you're wise. It's that kind of literature. So, we are using the word *fool* in the sense that the book of Proverbs does, and the Bible says this: "Do you see a man who is wise in his own eyes? There is more hope for a fool than for him" (Proverbs 26:12).

Can I quickly give you the characteristics of a fool, and then give you some hope, and then plunge into the Scriptures? What is the number one characteristic of a fool? You say, "You can't tell him anything." That's true, but why can't you tell a fool anything? I'll tell you exactly why. It's because he thinks he's wiser than you are. He doesn't know he's a fool. He doesn't know it. Denial isn't just a river in Egypt, you know. [*laughter*]. I mean he is living in a bubble. He's wiser than you are. Number one, he doesn't know he's a fool; and number two, therefore you can't tell him anything; and number three, he does the same thing over and over and over again without learning anything. That's what the book of Proverbs says the simpleton does.

Somebody gave this illustration. It's like having a hammer and you continue to hit your finger. You hit your finger and then you say to yourself, "You know I have a problem here. I have to change hammers. That's probably what my real problem is." And so you say to yourself, "I'm not getting along with this woman. What I really need is a new wife," and so you keep hitting yourself with a different hammer, but you're doing the same thing and not learning year after year after year. The book of Proverbs tells us a man like that is a fool.

I have a couple of comments. First of all, I need to emphasize that you marry the person you dated. Don't ever think you're going to change somebody. If he's an addict before you marry, I can assure you, he'll be a worse addict after you marry. I can assure you of that. If there is change, almost always it's for the worse and not the better. Don't ever marry somebody because you think you can change him or her. God might, but you can't. That's very, very important. In fact, during the dating experience, you actually see the nicest side of them, like a cartoon I once saw where a woman said, "Let's get married. I'm tired of being charming." [*laughter*] Or like advice given to young men—don't tell your girlfriend you're unworthy of her; let it come as a surprise. [*laughter*] You see them at their best, not at their worst.

Secondly, and this is important, if you didn't ignore some red flags, you probably never would've been married. Right? Didn't my wife ignore some red flags? I mean, how in the world—I'm speaking to the men now—did you get married if your wife didn't ignore some read flags? In fact, I'd like you to do something this afternoon if you're married. Look into the eyes of your wife and say, "Thank you for ignoring some red flags," and then she can thank you also, but don't get into an argument as to who ignored the most red flags. [*laughter*] All right? Don't go there. The simple fact is the world is broken. I'm going to be giving you a quote in another message that is chilling; [it's] by one of the Puritans about our sinfulness. You take this sinful person and this sinful person. Some of you are thinking "If I had married somebody else, I'd be happier." Don't be so sure.

I love to tell that story about a man who was walking through an asylum and there on the floor was a man who was beating his head against the wall (they had padded cells) saying, "Linda, how could you do it? Linda, how could you do it?" The man asked the director what was going on and he said, "He was madly in love with Linda and she jilted him and he couldn't take it. All he can do all day is hit his head against the wall and say, 'Linda, how could you do it?'" When they got to the end of the row, there was a man who was doing the same thing, pounding his head against the wall and saying, "Linda, how could you do it? Linda, how could you do it?" The man said, "What's that all about?" He said, "Well, he's the guy who married Linda." [*laughter*]

Folks, I have hope for you. Listen, my heart is filled today, and that's why we need to plunge into the Scriptures. I don't know if I can finish everything I've prepared. My heart is filled today with this fact, that no matter what situation you are in, no matter whom you married or wish you had married, or red flags you bypassed, I'm going to be telling you in the next message some red flags where a man married a woman and he had enough red flags to have his own parade, [*laughter*] but no matter where you are, you can glorify God in your response. Isn't that wonderful? [*applause*] Praise God.

Let's take our Bibles and turn to 1 Peter 3. I'll quickly give you an outline here about what's going on. The topic has to do with marriage and with women who are living with unsaved [husbands], as well as Christian husbands:

"Likewise, wives, be subject to your own husbands so that even if some do not obey the word, they may be won without a word by the conduct of their wives" (1 Peter 3:1).

If you're taking notes, number one, what the Bible says is, "Understand one another." Ladies, do you want to change your husband? Nagging won't do it. Judging won't do it. Cajoling won't do it. Trying to shame him won't do it. Why don't you let God do it? And how does God plan to do it? What is His plan? It is by the submission of the wives. Now this is such a huge topic, obviously we're going to be dealing with it later on in this series of messages, but I just need to say I've seen this time and time again.

I'm thinking of a situation where a man had a considerable amount of money, so he bought a considerable number of toys. I mean, we could say boats, cars, whatever, but his wife now began to spend even more than he, and she became very, very irrationally extravagant, and there was nothing he could say, and her big point was, "Well, you're doing it. Why can't I do it?" And pretty soon, what you have is a situation in which when he says "blue," she says "red." When he says "pink," she says "orange," and they can never get on the same page, because "I deserve this and I deserve that."

Listen, you can't have a happy marriage unless you obey God's Word, and the Bible says, "Wives, be submissive to your husbands." And that's a tough thing to say in today's culture. I understand how countercultural this is, but that is the means of God changing. Now, of course, if he's abusive— if he's abusing you or he's abusing the kids, then run—don't walk—to get help— but the point is that I can tell you story after story where there's no harmony because there's no submission, no willingness to sacrifice, and no willingness to "give up all my rights," which is our problem. It's my problem, it's your problem as sinful human beings. And as a result what do you get? You get conflict. There's always that undercurrent of conflict.

Now, on understanding one another, notice what it says in verse seven. It says, "Likewise, husbands, live with your wives in an understanding way" (1 Peter 3:7). You say, "Well, Pastor Lutzer, what does that mean?" Well, that's a long story, too, that we'll have to unpack in another message, but the fact is, many men don't take the time to try to understand their wives. They don't take the time to try to understand where they're coming from, and I know sometimes it is said that women can be unpredictable, and we know all of that, but we as husbands have the responsibility of understanding our wives—to walk in their shoes, so to speak, that we might get a handle on the kind of people and husbands we should be. There is to be understanding on both sides. Both sides need understanding.

And then we should, of course, understand one another, but now notice how he says, "Accept one another." I'm going to go here to 1 Peter 3:8. I know that here he's beginning another section. He's speaking to the whole church, but in speaking to the whole church, wouldn't this specifically relate to husbands and wives? Of course. Look at what he says, "Finally, all of you, have unity of mind." How in the world are you going to have unity when you disagree? Well, the answer is that there are some things you simply accept about your mate. You simply accept him or her even though you have those disagreements. But unity can be achieved without always agreeing on everything. She needs her space. You need your space. But it's very important though that you achieve that kind of unity.

Every once in a while, I have somebody say, "Oh, you know, we've been married for thirty years and we've never had an argument." Well, I admire a couple like that, but I can only tell you quite frankly, being married to Rebecca for forty years, our marriage wasn't quite that boring, if I might say that. [*laughter*] We all have our disagreements. We all argue from time to time and, God help us, may those instances become fewer and fewer. But the fact is, we need to be able to accept the differences as far as we are able, and have unity of mind even if, on all issues, we don't have exact agreement, and we accept our spouse with all of his or her failures and weaknesses even as we hope to be accepted ourselves with all of ours. The Bible says you achieve unity of mind so you are on the same page spiritually, the same page morally, and the same page in terms of your goals—and that becomes very critical.

What we should do is understand one another. We should accept one another, and now notice how Peter begins to talk about the emotional level of unity. He says, "sympathy, brotherly love, a tender heart, and a humble mind" (1 Peter 3:8). I'm going to kind of lump those together and simply say that we should have sympathy. I almost said symphony, and by the way, that wouldn't have been a bad mistake. That's what a symphony is all about. They're on the same page.

The Bible says we should have sympathy one to another. I don't think you can have unity simply on the intellectual level. What you need to do is enter into the other person's fears and anxieties and troubles, and when I read some of the other messages about red flags, you say, "Did you ever get any letters also from men?" The answer is yes and we'll share some of them with you. For us as men this is very difficult oftentimes to be that sympathetic listener and the person who cares. My wife, Rebecca, for the forty years we have been married, suffers from migraine headaches. As a matter of fact, she had a bad night last night though she is here today. I've often felt so guilty because I am not really able to enter into her pain, and I pray for her. Many years ago, I fasted for six days and had many concerns on my mind, but number one were her migraines, and God did not see fit to remove them from her. But my question is, "How can I enter into her world and bear her cross with her?" Which, by the way, she bears so marvelously. There are times when she has one of these migraines and I don't even know about it. But we as husbands need to have sympathy and be in symphony, I'll use both words, and begin to enter into one another's worlds.

Now, that is difficult. Husbands, you need to be able to listen to your wife. Don't simply be as one woman said, "I'm married to the great stone face. He's into the newspaper, he watches television, and there's no connection." You may eat together. You may go places together, but there's no emotional connection, and some of you, because of perhaps the way in which your wife has responded, maybe because of your background, you're finding it so difficult to connect on that level, but God expects us to. The Scripture speaks of "unity of mind, sympathy, brotherly love, a tender heart, and a humble mind" (1 Peter 3:8). Be quick to admit you're wrong. Be quick. Beat your wife (don't beat your wife; sometimes the lived event comes out differently than you're thinking). [*laughter*] Hurry to be faster than your wife—how does that sound?—to ask forgiveness.

And now we come to the biggie. Everything I've said up until now all comes together at this juncture. First Peter 3:9 says, "Do not repay evil for evil or reviling for reviling, but on the contrary, bless, for to this you were called, that you may obtain a blessing." Bless one another. Understand one another, and then we are also to be able to accept one another, have sympathy one to another and bless one another.

Here is where the rub comes. Notice it says do not render evil for evil. In a marriage relationship, or in any relationship, when you feel as if you have been sinned against, what do you and I naturally do? We sin back. "He does this; I'm going to show him a thing or two; I'm going to do that." And as a result, you have tension in this relationship because we think to ourselves that because he did this, I will do that, or vice versa. Having been sinned against, we sin. The Bible condemns that.

The best example of someone who was sinned against and didn't sin in return was Jesus, "who, when he was reviled, reviled not again; when he suffered, he threatened not; but committed himself to him that judgeth righteously" (1 Peter 2:23, KJV). Jesus is our example here, and you and I would not be redeemed today were it not for the fact that Jesus, when He was sinned against, refused to sin back. And if you're here today and you've never trusted Jesus as your Savior, that's why we offer you His redemption and His forgiveness. It's because He took what He didn't deserve so you and I might get what we don't deserve, namely His forgiveness and His righteousness. What a marvelous thing Jesus did for us, and you there in your guilt and in your despair and emptiness, I urge you today to trust in Jesus, who, when He was sinned [against] did not sin back.

But do you know what happens in marriages? You always find that people are more anxious to get even than they are to ask a different kind of question, namely, "How can I glorify God in the midst of this situation?" "My wife has done A, B, C, or D," you say. Or your husband has done these things, and rather than asking, "How do I get even? What do I do now? How do I straighten this out? How do I teach him a lesson?" you have a different question and that is, "How do I glorify God in the midst of this situation?" And when you begin to ask that question, you get different answers because you begin to understand no matter what mess you are in, today God has given to you as a child of God— as a daughter of God, as a son of God—the resources to respond in a godly way, and that's what God is looking for.

The issue isn't whether or not you straighten it out because you maintain your rights and you teach him (or you teach her). That's not the issue. The issue is how do we have godly responses when we're sinned against? To illustrate this, let me read a letter that was given to me some time ago in an entirely different context, and I'm reading it from the very sheet that was given to me. I read this letter because as you read it, you'll notice there were no red flags. He seemed to be marrying a very godly young woman, and yet things went very badly. But listen for this: Even though they went badly and he was greatly sinned against, he had an entirely different response.

"This is to Dr. Lutzer.

"I married a young woman nine years ago who had the same goal as me to be a foreign missionary. Two years later she gave birth to a severely disabled girl and our hopes of overseas missionary work were destroyed. What was worse was that my wife became so angry at God, that her heart turned against Him. On our six-year anniversary, she served me with divorce papers, and also revealed the identity of her new man that she was involved with, and eventually went on to move in with him, and later on to marry him. What is more, she moved my children (we have three) out of state to a location eleven hours away from me. When the children do come to visit me she does not send our handicapped daughter because of her distrust in my ability to care for her, which is totally unfounded. I have not had my daughter in my home for fourteen months. I know by all accounts, I have every right to be bitter with my ex-wife, however, I have made a promise to God that whatever happens to my ex, I will look out for her. I have always paid child support to her. Her current marriage is floundering and appears to be drawing to a close. She does not know this, but I have some potential business deals that may grant me outstanding financial returns. I have promised God that should she find herself destitute, I will not use it as a means to take our small children away from her like I know many others might do. I would rather provide her with whatever she needs to live. Obviously, I do not foresee ever reconciling with her to the point of remarrying, but I do pray that she finds the heart for serving God that she once had, and should she remarry, I pray that she finds a man who will stand as a godly example to the children. This is the most difficult resolution I have ever made in my life, and I don't boast in it in the least. It is not easy to maintain a positive attitude toward her, but God has given me the grace to make it, and it is making a world of difference in my life."

When we are sinned against, we glorify God best by not sinning in return. Let's pray.

I want to close in prayer, of course, but what has God said to you in this hurried message? Some of you perhaps are engaged, and based on this message, you see red flags all over the place. You should maybe rethink your impending marriage. We'll talk about that more next week.

Others of you know that there are huge issues in your marriage that just lie there unresolved. You don't want to touch them. Are you willing today to ask a different question? How can I glorify God in my marriage, rather than how can I maintain my rights, how can I do what is best for me? You talk to God right now if God has talked to you. I haven't talked to you. You've heard words, but only the Holy Spirit can take what I've said and bring it home into your life and give you the courage to be obedient. You talk to Him right now.

Father, we are so self-absorbed. We don't even see our sin. We see only our issues and our side of every story. It's tweaked to suit us. Would you come and reveal to us our sin that we might repent? But even those in a marriage who think they're the right one, may they be brought to repentance that, in humility and brokenness, you might give us sympathy for one another, that you might give us hearts that are forgiving. And may we never, never render evil for evil, but bless one another. Lord, you know all the couples listening to this who desperately need your intervention and help. Grant them the grace to let you do it. In Jesus' name, Amen.

SERMON TWO
MOVING BEYOND YOUR PAST

I believe the divorce many marriages experience already begins to take place before the wedding. Just like cracks on the tire of a car where you can predict a blowout, in the very same way, there are marriages that begin and you already know the pieces are in place for conflict, and probably eventually divorce. That's why I preached the last message on "Red Flags You Might Have Missed," but one of the red flags I didn't talk about, and we will talk about today, is the red flag of the past that the individuals bring to the relationship. If you don't know how to deal with your past, whatever that past may encompass, what you will do is bring to the marriage a body of death, and it will be as if death accompanies you for all the days you are together. It will always be there, and that is true if you are married, and of course, it is also true of your relationships if you are single. That's why this message is so important for you as well.

I need to tell you up front [that] some of the things I'm going to share with you today are going to be very difficult for some of you to receive. As a matter of fact, for some of you, this message will be something like having surgery without an anesthetic. It's going to be very painful. Some of you are going to react to what I have to say. You may even disagree. You may justify yourself and say, "He doesn't understand," but I believe that I do understand—not, of course, all situations. I'm simply saying that, in context, you'll accept these remarks as necessary to have a happy marriage.

I believe so deeply in this message. It is seldom that God begins to birth all of this burden in my heart early in the week, and yet that's the way this message has been. It has been in my soul Monday, Tuesday, Wednesday,

Thursday, Friday. I could hardly wait until Sunday. This could be a game changer for many of you. But in order that you might not just hear my words—because you can do that as you wish; you can take it or you can leave it—you need to hear the voice of God because some of the things I'm going to be saying, you will not see unless God shows them to you. It's not my message that will do it, and it's not as if this message is the beginning and end of all that you need to know about a happy marriage. It is only one piece along the journey, and we all need to hear it, and so this is what I would like to do.

Knowing this may be a tough thirty minutes, if you as a husband are here today and you are sitting next to your wife, could I ask you to take her hand? I want you to take her hand because we're going to pray, and I want you as a husband to pray quietly in your heart that as a result of this message, your good marriage will be better, and your bad marriage will be made good.

Let's bow together in prayer.

Father, who is sufficient for these things? Who can hear what we have to say? Who can understand the pain some people will feel and the discomfort over what will be said? And yet, Lord, we thank you that you always cut us that you might heal us. You wound us, not to destroy us but to heal us so that we can be better used by you. We ask that whatever preconceptions are brought to this that you might indeed help those to be put aside as we hear not my voice which is powerless, but the voice of Almighty God. We pray in Jesus' name, Amen.

What are some of those pasts that people bring to their marriage? Well, of course, one of the most obvious is the past of expectations. That is to say, if you're brought up in a certain home and your father acted in such a way, or you didn't have a father and you didn't know how fathers should act, you have a certain image in your mind as to how your husband is going to act, how your wife is going to act, and you suddenly discover different backgrounds, different aspirations, different expectations. Certainly, unrealistic expectations is one of the disappointments of marriage. People come to marriage expecting marriage to do only what God can, and so they're disappointed three months or a year into the relationship.

But let me hurry on to something that is even more difficult that we bring to our marriages, and that is the baggage of the past, the wounds other people have inflicted on us. Today, I am speaking to some of you who were brought up in a home where there was alcoholism and your father beat you, and as a result of that kind of experience, you have certain expectations, certain feelings about men, certain feelings about life, and you bring to the marriage a very open wound. Some of you have been sexually molested. If it's true that one out of every four girls born is going to be molested, then the number of women who have experienced sexual abuse of some kind at the hand of someone else is huge. Obviously hundreds [of abused people] are probably listening to me right now. If you don't know how to take care of that, what will happen is you will bring to your marriage an open wound.

When you marry, you are going to be saying to your spouse in effect, "I want you to heal me. Heal my wound, but don't you dare touch *that* wound, because if you touch it, not only will I holler, not only will I criticize you, but eventually, I will divorce you to find someone who can really understand me, who can really heal my wound." So, what you're doing is asking your mate to do something no mate can do. He can help. She can help. But in the end, it's something only God can do, and your expectations are too high. And if you remain wounded, and the wound remains open, you will set up circumstances in such a way that your mate will never please you.

If I might use this illustration, a man might think to himself, "I finally have my wife figured out. I finally know what will please her," and he discovers even if he can't get a touchdown, at least he can kick a field goal. But while the ball is in the air, the goal posts move, and he discovers that's not the right thing anyway, and again he is back to square one. So we bring to it the wounds others have inflicted on us.

The third thing we bring to marriage is the sin that we personally have committed—our "poor choices," as it is called today—our sins. Of course, I could speak of many, but because sexuality is such a great part of us, I'm going to be speaking about sexual sin. The Bible, in 1 Corinthians 6, gives us more information regarding the sexual experience than all the books that have ever been written by human philosophers.

The Bible says that he who is joined to a harlot is one body with her. Now just think about that. Here's a relationship that is not based on love, it is lust for money. It is the most debased sexual relationship you can think of, and God says, "I put them together and they become one body." Metaphysically they are joined. The intention of God, of course, is that you be joined to the one you marry, and you be joined after you marry her or him, and therefore you have this unique relationship. But according to a book I read yesterday, only twenty percent of those in the evangelical churches in America come to the altar with both being virgins.

What you have is a situation in which this young man has been joined to this woman, this girl. She, perhaps, has been joined to all these guys. And now they come together and we expect them to live happily ever after, and they've not really dealt with their past in a very satisfying way. As a result of that, there is a tendency to promiscuity that will develop later on, once the marriage becomes an average marriage, maybe even a boring marriage. But also what is going to happen is that young people like that find it very difficult to commit. They can't commit because they can't trust themselves; like one man said, "I've had so many relationships I can't commit." He said, "I'd like to be true to one person, but I don't see how I can."

And so what you bring is all of that baggage, enough to fill a Pullman freight car, and now suddenly you're supposed to be happy when there's a little bit of you left with this person, and a little bit with this person, and a little bit with that, and here you are. By the way—parenthesis—never get married to someone with whom you are having an active sexual relationship. If you want to be married, live apart for at least six months—we have that rule here at The Moody Church as pastors—so you can prove there is something more to this relationship than trying to take a defiled bed and turn it into an undefiled one. But this is brought to our marriages today, so what do we do? I'm so glad you asked because that's exactly the same page that I'm on.

First of all, it is so important for us to take responsibility. You have to "own your stuff," as the saying goes, and that is critical. Let me give David in the Old Testament as an example. This is a classic. David commits adultery. He steals a man's wife, and then he kills her husband to cover it up. It's pretty serious stuff. David begins to live month after month hoping it will pass by. He's thinking, "If I give this enough time, it will work itself out." He's a typical man. By the way, there are some of you who think I am harder on the men than I am on the women. I don't think you're going to say that by the time this message ends, but anyway, he was a typical man. You know, "Just give me enough time; okay I messed up, but let's get on with life." He says in Psalm 32, that day and night, God's hand was heavy upon him, and so he was feeling conviction, but you know, it's going to blow over. Typical.

Nathan, the prophet, comes and says, "David, I want to tell you about what's just happened in your kingdom. There was a wealthy man with all kinds of sheep, and then there was a poor man who had only one small sheep that he took care of and a man came to the wealthy man and said, 'May I stay here?' And the wealthy man went and stole the poor man's sheep. What do you think should be done?" And the Bible says that David's anger was kindled against the man and he said, "He deserves to die but make sure that he pays back fourfold." Nathan said, "David, you are the man" (2 Samuel 12:7).

David was more concerned, get this, over somebody stealing somebody's lamb than he was about him stealing a wife who didn't belong to him and then committing murder to cover it up. Folks, where sin is viewed superficially, it is dealt with superficially. [You need to be] willing to take out the time to say, "I have to own my stuff and I have to feel the full import of my sin." David not only minimized his sin in the sight of God, but [also] in the sight of others. We always minimize our sin in the sight of others. It is human nature.

Do you remember that, last time, I told you about narcissists? The thing about a narcissist is not just that he's into himself. He doesn't care how he hurts those around him, and that's the way David was until, in that same chapter, he says finally, "I have sinned," and then when he pours out his heart in Psalm 51, he uses the word *I* or *me* about six times in five verses. "Have mercy on me, O God, according to your steadfast love; according to your abundant mercy blot out my transgressions. Wash me thoroughly from my iniquity, and cleanse me from my sin!" (Psalm 51:1–2).

David finally got it, and I am here today to ask you, "Have you gotten it or are you simply dealing with it superficially?" [Are you saying,] "Okay, okay, I messed up already"? Sin is serious. Do you know the extent to which you have hurt the heart of your wife or the heart of your husband? We have to own our own stuff.

Secondly, what we need to do is to accept God's forgiveness. I'm going to skip over this because, in a sense, that's the easy part, even though it is difficult. But we don't have time to go into it all the way, but I'm going to jump to number three.

Number three, we have to clear our own consciences. This is what the Bible says in 1 Timothy 1:5. It says we should have love flowing "from a pure heart and a good conscience." If you don't have a good conscience, you don't have a good marriage, and I don't care how hard you try.

Let me give you examples, and they are all true, of marriages with bad consciences. A wife confesses to me and says, "I am cheating on our checkbook. My husband's so stingy and I cheated on the checkbook because I took money from the account that he doesn't know about and now I'm thinking payday is coming." How can she have a good conscience? She can't.

There are women who have had abortions their husbands don't know about. There are husbands who have had affairs their wives don't know about. I read about one woman yesterday who said, "I could handle it if it were an affair with a woman, but it happens to be with a man," but even for that, there is hope.

Then you have all of these issues. I think, for example, of a man who walks with God. He's pursuing God with all of his heart. He's in fellowship with God. He is well-versed in the Scripture, but whenever he is asked to do something ("Would you become an elder?" "Would you be a Sunday school teacher?"), "No, no, no." He disqualifies himself because (nobody knows this except he confessed to a friend of mine) he has a child, a boy, growing up in Houston because of a premarital relationship he had, a fleeting relationship in college. And his wife and kids don't know about it, and you see, every time he wants to walk with God, there it is. How can you walk with God? Look at your past. You have to clear your conscience, and the best way to do that is always with someone, especially if it's a huge issue.

If you were to ask me what is the most memorable counseling experience, if I could put it that way, I've ever had, I would tell you, hands down, it was when a wife asked me to sit in with her husband as she confessed to him that their third child was not his. These are tough situations, but you see, she was driven to mental illness, trying to cope with the guilt, trying to live with an unclear conscience.

Let me ask you something, husband over there. How can you and I love our wives, get it now, when love, the Bible says, "springs from a pure heart and a good conscience," when you've got all this stuff going on, on the side over there, [that] she doesn't know about? (Or that he doesn't know about?) How can you do it? You can't.

Let's go on to the next point, and that is we are to forgive as we have been forgiven. If you want to, you can take your Bibles at this point and turn to the passage of Scripture in Ephesians 4. I'm going to begin at verse 29. It says, "Let no corrupting talk come out of your mouths, but only such as is good for building up, as fits the occasion, that it may give grace to those who hear. And do not grieve the Holy Spirit of God, by whom you were sealed for the day of redemption." And what grieves the Spirit? There it is: "Let all bitterness and wrath and anger and clamor and slander be put away from you, along with all malice. Be kind to one another, tenderhearted, forgiving one another, as God in Christ forgave you" (Ephesians 4:29–32).

So, if it is true that you and I are supposed to forgive as we've been forgiven, the question then is, "How does God forgive?" Well, first of all, He does forgive big sins. We all know that, but secondly, when He forgives, the sin is not held against us anymore. Now some of the consequences are there, absolutely, but the sin itself is put away. It's covered. The Bible says it is covered, it is cast into the depths of the sea (Psalm 103:12). It is taken and removed as far as the east is from the west, so God says, "That's not going to be an issue between us anymore. You know the sin you committed? We can still be in fellowship now because I've put it away." All right? You got it?

Now the question is, how do we forgive? Now here's what happens and here's where it's going to get very difficult. If you come to your marriage with a wound and you have never forgiven those who have wronged you, and you've never really received God's forgiveness for the sins you have committed, what you will do is you will not forgive as you've been forgiven. If you want to keep the wound and you don't want to be healed (and there are many people out there who don't want to be) what's going to happen is this: You are going to live out of your woundedness. It is going to become your identity. It is going to become who you are. It is going to become your calling card because you absolutely refuse to forgive, which [forgiveness] is the only way that wounds can be healed.

Let me give you an example. Rebecca and I know a woman who has been divorced twice and has a number of children, and the way in which she reacted to her woundedness (apparently by her father—some abuse was going on there; and then, of course, she was misused by husbands and all that. It's a long story) is she parented her children out of her wound. So what did she do (because the desire of wounded people is to control those around them)? She overcorrected her children. I mean, those kids couldn't sniffle without her getting onto them. "We're not going to do that in this house. This house is going to...etc." Lady, you are parenting out of your wound.

See, that's why the Bible says beware "lest a root of bitterness springing up trouble you and thereby many be defiled." If you forget everything I've said to you today, and I'm pouring my heart out to you, will you remember that whatever you do not forgive, you pass on. Therefore she passes on her woundedness and her resentment. Now, if you were to talk to her and say, "You know, lady, you're overcorrecting because of your wound. You want to control and you don't have a husband to control anymore so now you're controlling the children" would she say, "Thank you for pointing that out. That is really good. I appreciate that"? No, this has been her identity for thirty–forty years. This is who she is. You can't be with her for ten or fifteen minutes without her telling you about her woundedness. This is who she is. She is her wound. She doesn't see it. [She would say,] "You just don't understand the depth of my pain."

Folks, I understand it may take years to overcome some things, but if you're old enough to be married, you're old enough to finally, once and for all, lay it down, but she won't because it is her identity. That's what it's become.

Let me give you another example. Many years ago, I was preaching in Florida, and I don't know what I was preaching on, but a man and I struck up a conversation, and he said to me, "Twenty years ago I had a very brief, fleeting affair, and because I'm a Christian, I confessed it to my wife, and she professed to forgive me, but to this day she still rubs my nose in the dirt." Very interesting.

I have to ask you a question. When that dear lady goes out with her friends, what do you think she says to them? Does she say, "You know, twenty years ago, my husband had an affair and it really gave me power. With it I can win any argument because I can always remind him. In fact, I don't even have to remind him because it's always there. It's always understood. When he asks me to do something I don't want to do, I don't have to do it because he knows right well he owes me. As a matter of fact, not only does he owe me then, but let's suppose he's doing something I don't like, I can lord it over him. I can control him. There is nothing he has done in our marriage that has so empowered me." Is that what she says? Of course not.

I'm making this up because I don't know all the circumstances, but I know human nature enough to know that's probably what's happening. But no, what she actually says is, "You know, my husband had an affair twenty years ago, and I forgave him, but you know we're still working through our issues." That's what she would say to them, but actually it's her means of control, control, control.

Why is it that these people don't just simply give it up? It is because of loss of control. Think of what would happen. You see, she doesn't have to respect her husband even though the Bible commands her to. Who can respect a man like that? You ask, "Well, do these ladies pray for their husbands?" Of course, they pray for them. And what I'm saying about the ladies, by the way, can also be said about the men. You understand that. But of course, they do. They're always enlisting God's help to bring about a change in their husbands they would like to see, and they want God to be their companion in chipping him into the man he should be, and the wastebaskets in heaven seem to be filled with all kinds of unanswered prayers that the angels take and burn with the trash, if there is such a thing in heaven. Because the one thing she will not do is to simply give her husband to God, to trust God for him, to trust that if he is unfaithful or something, God will reveal it to her. God can do that in many different ways. Respect him and speak well of him—that she will not do.

Like it was said of one couple, "Oh, they buried the hatchet, but the grave was shallow and well-marked." And so they keep going to that grave and, I might add, that when you looked at it, you could see a pathway made to it. Power. I've got it over you. So, what you need to do is to lay it down.

Now, if you're thinking with me, and I believe you are, you have a question. Always be asking questions while I'm preaching. I'm sometimes doing that, too, while I'm preaching. You've heard about the preacher who dreamt he was preaching and then he woke up and found out he was. [*laughter*] So if you're tracking with me, you have another question and that is: "Okay, all right, you have my number. How do I lay it down?" Well, we've talked about the cleansing of the conscience, which oftentimes should be done with someone else present—a pastoral staff member, an elder—especially in some of these really hard things, some of which I've outlined. But then let me give you some very important steps of what you need to do.

First of all, I think what you need to do is to get over this idea that you don't have to forgive unless you feel like it. I heard a counselor say that one time, and I strongly disagree. Of course you can't forgive right away in the sense that here you have this injustice— if somebody were to rape one of your children you wouldn't say, "Oh well, you know, he did it this morning, but by evening we've forgiven." No, no, no. I understand it takes time. I understand the healing process. I know these things aren't just so nicely cut and dry, but there does come a time when you as an adult, walking with God, choose to put it down whether you feel like it or not. Force yourself to, because it's biblical.

The Bible says to forgive others. Of course I know when there's unfaithfulness, there has to be a time not only of forgiveness but the rebuilding of trust. I get all that, but I'm talking about you.

You dear single mothers, God bless you. God bless the single mothers. I'm so glad we have a class for them here at The Moody Church. I plead with you: Do not parent out of your woundedness. That little boy who looks so much like the man you are tempted to hate, don't hate him, but love him and learn to parent not out of woundedness but out of wholeness, and you can't do it without forgiveness.

What I'm asking you to do today is like crawling through the eye of a needle. It's that hard, but it has to be done. There is no other way. This may be surgery without anesthetic, but you've got to do it.

By the way, don't ever think that if [you] forgive, somehow it lessens the horror of what was done. That's such a big mistake. Come to the conclusion that all rational people should come to—that the harm that the bitterness is doing to you is much greater than it is to the person who victimized you or the person who took advantage of you, and in the name of Jesus, lay it down. In fact, that's what I'd like to say. If the first step is to choose to do it, the second is to simply say, "I take a good look at it. I have camped here. I have lived here. This has been my life-blood and my woundedness, and in the name of Jesus, I want to pour it out at the foot of the cross because I want my wound to become a scar."

Scars are great. Jesus will have a scar in heave. A scar means there's been healing. It's a reminder of the fact of where you've been, but a scar means I can move on. I don't have to be dragging this dead body into our marriage and carrying it around year after year, and so what you do is you take a good look at it, and in some instances, weep for your past. I mean, if you lost an arm, you would have no problem weeping over that. Why not weep over a lost childhood if that's what it takes?

But then third, be sure you substitute your own wounds with the wounds of Jesus. The Bible says in Isaiah 53:5, "He was wounded for our transgressions, he was bruised for our iniquities: the chastisement of our peace was upon him; and with his stripes (with his wounds) we are healed" (NIV).

You say, "Well, Pastor Lutzer, how does that work?" Well, the answer is this: Through His wounds, Jesus took what He didn't deserve, namely our sin. Remember the words of the beautiful song by Charles Wesley?

"Five bleeding wounds He bears,
received on Calvary;
they pour effectual prayers,
they strongly plead for me.
'Forgive him, O, forgive,' they cry,
'Nor let that ransomed sinner die!'"

Jesus took what He didn't deserve, namely our sin. You say, "My husband doesn't deserve forgiveness," or you say, "My wife doesn't deserve forgiveness." That's not the issue. Nobody deserves it, but the Bible says Jesus died on the cross, so Jesus got what He didn't deserve—our sin, and now we, in turn, get what we don't deserve, namely His forgiveness and His righteousness as belonging to us. What a glorious exchange! Jesus said, "Now that I can forgive you freely, now that your sin no longer needs to be an issue between you and me, why don't you forgive as you have been forgiven? Begin to live your life through the prism not of your woundedness, but of my woundedness." Because ultimately, He bore not only our sins, the Bible says He also bore our sorrows. There at the foot of the cross, thanking God for what was done for us in Jesus, we discover that if Jesus was willing to do that for us when we were yet enemies, why can't I exercise the same grace to somebody who has victimized me? His wounds were not self-inflicted. His wounds were inflicted by evil men, and out of those wounds, scars developed which we're going to see in heaven because it says, "I saw as it were a lamb that had been slain." I expect in heaven to see the wounds of Jesus, but they'll not be wounds— I should clarify that— but scars. And you'll be there too, maybe with your scars, but the wounds will be gone. Trust Jesus.

Then finally, develop a different pattern of thought. Just like the needle of a compass points north when it's free, in the same way, some of you, when your mind is free, allow it to go back to your woundedness. It goes back to your self-pity. "Poor me. Look at the husband I married. I could have done much better if I had shopped more wisely." It doesn't matter. We're talking about both men and women here, and when you stop to think of it, folks, what happens is, these thought patterns are so strongly ingrained that you have to begin to think differently.

Those of you who are older all know who Jim Bakker was and is—the Jim Bakker of the great television scandals in the middle of the 1980s, who then went to jail, and in fact, has a new ministry today. About five years ago,

Rebecca and I were in Branson and we had lunch with Jim Bakker and his wife, Lori. Tammie Faye, of course, died, but Lori is his new wife, and she gave us a book of her story, and she told us her story. I don't even remember the number of abortions this young lady had before the age of twenty. Every sin imaginable, whether it's drugs and sex and booze—you name it, this girl was into it, but she was gloriously converted. And I remember this, she said, "I memorized 400 verses of Scripture just to get my mind straight." Today she is a lovely woman and deeply in touch with those who ache and hurt and are wounded—because she's been there. You need to think differently.

Now listen, you also need to speak differently. If your Bible is open like mine is, did you notice what I read in Ephesians 4:29? "Let no corrupting talk come out of your mouths, but only such as is good for building up, as fits the occasion." Oh, if we could take that one verse and implement it in our marriages, it would change everything. Let me tell you a true story.

A woman plans to divorce her husband within a month. The attorney says, "Okay, you're going to divorce the guy anyway. He doesn't know you're going to divorce him, and you basically hate him, but in order to hurt him more, so you can really sock it to him, why don't you, for one month, do nothing but commend him and say nice things about him and encourage him and respect him? He will think you're really on his side, and then when you serve him the divorce papers it will hurt a whole lot more." She loved the idea. There's no use criticizing the guy. You're going to lose him anyway. I mean, you know, he's going to be out of here, so forget about all of his faults and all of the things you don't like about him. Give him love notes in his lunch. Say nice things. If he does something sensible, commend him for it (and ladies, that would be a wonderful thing for you to do for your husbands, is to commend him if he does something sensible).

Somebody here at the church asked me one time if a man speaks and his wife isn't there to hear him, is he still wrong? [*laughter*]

So [this woman] did nothing but speak positive things to him for one whole month. Seriously, at the end of the month, they went on a second honeymoon.

Can you imagine what that would do? The Bible says, "Speak words that edify." Could you make a promise right now? Rebecca and I talked about this, so we're in on the promise. For one full week—168 hours, I actually calculated it on my calculator, there will be no criticism. Oh, you might want to tell him before he goes to work there is some porridge on his shirt or something like that— that may not be a criticism. Correcting something might not be a criticism, but no criticism, no nagging. All day long, what you're thinking about as a wife and as a husband is, "How can I speak words that will uplift, words that will edify? How can I do that?" and your marriage will be transformed absolutely. There's no doubt about it.

Ladies and men, it can be done by the power of God, but if not, we grieve the Spirit. How big is God? Here's David. He commits his sin. He messes up his family. He has Bathsheba for a wife. She bears him Solomon. We could argue that, strictly speaking, Solomon should never have been born because he was born to a woman who should never have been David's wife, and lo and behold Solomon is born, and the Bible says, "And the LORD loved him" (2 Samuel 12:24). And the Lord said to him, I will bless you "for the sake of your father, David," and I just look at that and say, "Where's all that coming from?" It's coming from grace because, do you know what God does with our past when we deal with it? He recycles it and makes it come out to His glory.

Another true story. Solomon's story is true and this one is also. I have a friend, whom I shall call Ken, though he wouldn't mind, I'm sure, if I told you his real name. I think he shares his story freely. There he is. He's brought up and, early in life, he comes to know Christ as Savior. At the age of twenty-five, his mother sets him down and says, "I have something to share with you. The person whom you think is your father is not your father. I had a fleeting affair with a doctor in the area and he's your biological dad."

Now Ken, at that moment, had two ways he could go. He could've said, "I'm going to go into drugs and into alcohol and the whole bit because, after all, I shouldn't have even been here. I need validation as a human being. I don't even know whether or not I was the product of any kind of love, or whether or not it was just a fleeting, lustful relationship. I don't even know who I am." He could have done that but he was a Christian and he believed the Bible. What a wonderful combination!

The Bible says where sin abounds, grace abounds much more. So after being thrown for a loop for a while, trying to get his bearings as to what this means as to who he is, after going through that, he decided if God was big enough to save me, why can't He be big enough to bless me? After all, God has chosen him and made him a son of God, [and had] forgiven his sin. His position in heaven is secure. I'd say that's validation. It's pretty good for a guy who, strictly speaking, could have argued he should not have been born. Why? It's because God is so much bigger than your sin.

I believe Spurgeon was right when he said, "The abundance of sin can never thwart the abundance of grace." Spurgeon said, "Man heaps a pile of sin, and God says, 'I'm going to do you better. I'm going to heap a pile of grace that is bigger.' Man says, 'Mine is going to be even bigger yet,' and God comes along and He heaps a whole mountain of grace and says, 'Mine is bigger,'" and on and on it goes until man loses the contest because God's grace is greater than your sin and greater than your past. [*applause*] To those who receive it, God's grace is great.

I don't know where you are in your marriage. All I know is if we humbled ourselves, repented and owned our stuff, and cleared our consciences, and then really forgave, and began to speak differently, we'd be on a different course.

We all know about the story of Corrie ten Boom in a concentration camp in Nazi Germany. Her sister was killed by the Nazis. She [Corrie] survived the camp and then blessed us with her book she wrote. Later on, she met one of the Nazis in the concentration camp where she was and he stuck out his hand (this is here in America) to her. She didn't know whether or not she should take it, but she thought, "If God is this gracious to me to forgive me, I'll shake hands with him," and then she said these words I'll never forget. "There is no pit so deep but that God is deeper still." You're not in a pit that is so deep but that God is deeper.

Let's pray.

So, where do we go from here? You husbands especially, I want you to pray and take the hand of your wife like I asked you to do when we prayed earlier. Don't accuse one another as a result of this message. The devil would like that. Satan has some of you bound in unbelief and bound in your woundedness, but God is here to deliver. Would you talk to God right now as we have a moment of silent prayer?

Father, we've said the words, but will they be heard? Will that man have the courage to do what he needs to do? Will that wife have the courage to do what she needs to do? Will they see their sin, as all of us need to? Will they see your grace as greater than the sin? I don't know, because this is your work. It's not mine. I pray you might bring many miracles about, many miracles of restoration and hope. Do that, Lord, we pray. Amen.

SERMON THREE

THE PUZZLE OF YOUR ROLES

I begin today with a question: What is a woman and what is a man? What is masculinity and what is femininity? That's the question we hope to solve in the next few moments, and solve them based on the Bible.

Many of you know this is the third in a series of messages entitled, *The Marriage Puzzle,* and it is a puzzle, isn't it?

Some time ago this summer, I asked if people would write down red flags they missed during their dating years before they were married. What red flag did you overlook that became a problem later in the marriage? Some of you will know that in the first message in this series I delineated four red flags, and today I'm going to give you one more. Here are two letters I received from women who married a mama's boy.

"My husband could do nothing without asking his mother. She either came with us or he got permission from her to go anywhere. He was nearly thirty when we dated and I saw the writing on the wall. Well, during the honeymoon, he was constantly checking with his mother about everything. We've been married fifteen years and have a lot of grief in our marriage. We've had difficulty with my mother-in-law." Really? "in setting boundaries for her. He was in an enmeshing and controlling family and he failed to leave and cleave." But notice this. "It took the grace of God and counseling to overcome this obstacle in our marriage. Even today we have to deal with the weeds in the garden of our relationship, but we are facing them with a united front. We can see how gracious God was in protecting our marriage from divorce, and together we are learning to rejoice in God."

So that's a success story, but here's another like it.

"We've been married for seventeen years and are still struggling with the issue of boundaries and bitterness. For the first twelve years of our marriage, my husband spent more time worrying about his mother's feelings than mine. He was raised without a dad and no other siblings, but his mother seems to be his ex-wife to me, and although he has changed, we are now believers, I have a hard time trusting that he puts me first."

Well, what do we have to say to mama's boy? Before this message is over I'll have some words for him.

What is a man? What is a woman? I think it is true to say most women have a better idea of who they are than most men. Men don't know who they are and who they're supposed to be, and let me tell you why. First of all, I think it's because of the feminization of our culture. You know, we were told if you give boys dolls, they will play with dolls just like girls do because it's all conditioning. So, they gave boys dolls and discovered that they bent them into the shape of a gun [*laughter*] and then they began to realize maybe there is a fundamental difference between boys and girls.

Now, of course, all of us would agree that women should have equal pay for equal work. We agree that they are equal in terms of value and, oftentimes, superior in intelligence. We agree with that, but the feminist movement overreached; and by overreaching, it confused, in a very serious way, the roles of men and women. And because of this, men don't know who they are because they thought all the roles are interchangeable, and they aren't. Intrinsic to every man and every woman are certain dispositions, as we shall see, and while they may do a number of different things, the fact is femininity and masculinity lie at the heart of who we are as persons. But men today don't know who they should be. If they hold back, they are wimps. If they give leadership, then they are insensitive. So who should they be?

Another reason for this is because pornography has deadened the desire of some men for romance. As a result, you find today that for men who have seen everything and perhaps done everything, the mystique is gone. But perhaps the most important reason is the breakup of the family. With the family broken up and so many homes without a father, boys grow up not knowing who they are, and not knowing how a father should act. They bond with their mothers. And girls grow up and they, of course, want to fall into the arms of the first boy who tells them they are beautiful, because there's no dad there to affirm them and to give them the guidelines and to know where the boundaries are. Consequently, we are in trouble today in our families.

The result of all of this is that men (and this may also be true of women) first of all, are really hesitant to commit. I know there are some women who feel as if young men today date young women, and they build friendships, and the young woman makes a tremendous investment (maybe of months and years) in the relationship, and then the guy just walks away as if nothing happened. He is either unaware of how deeply he has hurt her or else he doesn't care, and so we live in a day of what we could call "disposable relationships."

One young woman said to me, "We are like cars in a parking lot, and guys come along and they test drive this car, and then they test drive that car, but they aren't interested in commitment. They're interested in a friendship that can be disposed of when it is convenient." That's one of the problems of our culture.

Yet another reason [that men don't know who they are] is that you find a boy sometimes is trapped in a man's body. The guy simply never grew up, and even though he should be an adult, he doesn't act like one. Somehow his childhood got missed along the way and, of course, he gets married because he's interested in sex, but he becomes very bored with that after a while and he is unwilling to do the hard work of having a good marriage. One time I heard someone say when he was divorcing one wife to marry another woman, "You know, I work hard all day. I figure I shouldn't have to come home and work on my marriage." Well, sorry, but if you don't work on your marriage it isn't going to be a good one. Rebecca and I actually know a woman who told us her husband still played with toy boats in the bathtub. Some just have not grown up. [*laughter*] Yeah, that's true.

In years gone by, it seems to me, men were men and women were women, and everyone knew where they fit. It seems to me that's the way it used to be, but it isn't now. I think Jesus was a real man. I think when Jesus was walking by the Sea of Galilee and He saw these real men who would become His disciples, fishing, He was able to speak to them in such a confident way that they were willing to put down their nets and follow Him. Today, you can't get some men to put down their remote and come to church. And by the way, do you know why it is that men love the remote control so much? It's because to a man, even remote control is better than none at all. [*laughter*]

Now, the question is: What is a man and what is a woman? I'm going to take the definition of John Piper, and this is based on the Word of God and not on contemporary culture. John Piper says, "At the heart of a mature masculinity is a sense of benevolent responsibility"—notice these words—"to lead, provide for, and protect women in ways appropriate to a man's different relationships." That's the heart of a mature man. It's a sense of benevolent responsibility to lead, provide for, and to protect women. That's the way in which God wired us.

Of course, there are many women who don't know who they are either, and they don't know who they are because they grew up in a culture where beauty was everything. Young girls, who are now mothers, grew up during the days when Madonna was popular, so they've come through that phase. Of course, the contemporary ones are into Britney Spears or Paris Hilton, and some of these role models (if you can use that word), and as a result, they grow up thinking they have value only if they are pretty and beautiful, and as a result, [they have] all kinds of insecurities and all kinds of marital problems.

Rebecca and I know of two instances where wives (mothers) have left their children behind. Now this is even contrary to natural desire and natural affection. They've left their children and they have gone out to seek other men because they constantly need the approval of other men. They have an insatiable desire because they don't know who they are either. What a mess, and what a world in which we live, and the media certainly is partially responsible.

Let me give you a definition of femininity. This also is John Piper's definition: "At the heart of mature femininity is a freeing disposition to affirm, receive, and nurture strength and leadership from worthy men in ways appropriate to a woman's different relationships." The key words there are affirm, receive, and nurture strength, and so that is part of her DNA, or part of her hard wiring.

This summer, when I asked people to write to me and to tell me the red flags they missed, I [received] this note scribbled on the back of an envelope, and I want to read it to you because you can understand [that] marriage sometimes represents the perfect storm, doesn't it? You've got all of these insecurities, all of these misconceptions on one side, and all of the expectations and misconceptions on the other side, and then you put them together and they're supposed to live happily ever after. This is what some anonymous person (with a lot of insight) wrote:

He said, "Love is blind by design. Why else would you marry this person who is completely different, with different parents, a completely different DNA, with radically different expectations, and with radically different life experiences? Why would you do this for marital bliss?" He says, "You only do it because love is blind or," he says, "is all of this possibly a total setup by the sovereign hand of an all-wise God? Perhaps this very one we have married is chosen by God himself, chosen because this is the person through whom He would chasten, scourge, and humble us, as a means to conform us to the very image of Christ so that we would come forth as gold."

I think he was onto something. Don't you agree with that? Remember this: In marriage you have the vanity of a woman, you have the ego of a man, and surgery is done on both without anesthetic. There you are under 24-hour surveillance with all of your faults, all of your insecurities, and with nowhere to hide. It's just you, and what an experience it is.

I think at this point, it's time for us to turn to the Scriptures and to see who God says we are, and to confirm our understanding of femininity and masculinity. The passage of Scripture is the second chapter of the book of Genesis; Genesis 2, the creation account. What you need to do is to go back to the original manual.

Have you ever tried to put a bicycle together? I think I tried that one time and I discovered I couldn't do it. I thought, "Well, all the pieces are there. You just somehow know this piece fits there and this one goes there," and then you discover it's so complicated that maybe I should look at the manual. The Bible is God's manual. If we want to know how it is to be put all together and how the pieces should fit, it's all here.

First of all, in this account I want you to notice how God did it. Let's look at the creation, the materials themselves. Genesis 2:7 says, "Then the LORD God formed the man of dust from the ground and breathed into his nostrils the breath of life, and the man became a living creature." God just went and made a mud man, and then He breathed life into him. Ladies, don't you think you expect too much from us, considering our origin? [*laughter*] We're made from mud, but that's not true of women.

It is very interesting what the Bible says. Genesis 2:18 says, "Then the LORD God said, 'It is not good that the man should be alone.'" That's amazing. He [Adam] is in paradise with everything he could possibly want, and God said it was not good for him to be alone. Adam had desires that nothing else could possibly fulfill, and then Scripture says, "Now out of the ground the LORD God had formed every beast of the field and every bird of the heavens and brought them to the man to see what he would call them." Well, that's interesting. I thought God was making a helpmeet for him. "And whatever the man called every living creature, that was its name. The man gave names to all livestock and to the birds of the heavens and to every beast of the field. But for Adam there was not found a helper fit for him" (Genesis 2:19–20). None of the animals could satisfy the desires of Adam's heart.

"So," the Bible says, "the LORD God caused a deep sleep to fall upon the man, and while he slept took one of his ribs and closed up its place with flesh. And the rib that the LORD God had taken from the man he made into a woman and brought her to the man" (Genesis 2:21–22).

Man was made from inorganic material—mud, but the woman is made out of organic material because she's going to be the mother of all living. Notice, though, that what God did is He separated femininity out of masculinity. He took and made the woman out of the man and then He implanted within them a strong, unrelenting desire to come back to one another and to be intimately related and connected—and that also lies at the heart of all femininity and masculinity. And so the LORD God said, right from the creation, that woman was to come out of the man and she would be the mother of all living, the Scripture says.

Let's look at the way in which God did it. You'll notice in verse seven it says the LORD God took man and He made him from the dust of the ground; God just made this man and breathed life into him (Genesis 2:7). Actually, in Hebrew, there is a different word when it comes to woman. This is not reflected in our translation we have, but many of the translations translate it more accurately when they say from the rib the LORD God "fashioned" a woman. He *made* man but He *fashioned* a woman, and I think the whole idea there is that a woman, being fashioned, is a work of art. I mean, we as men are just kind of thrown together and given life. Women are beautiful and symmetrical. The LORD God made Eve that way. No wonder the Bible says that Adam said, "This at last is bone of my bones and flesh of my flesh" (Genesis 2:23). I'm sure he said some other things, too, as God brought her to him.

Now let's look at the details in terms of the roles the men and the women should have. What are some of the roles as indicated here? There are different ways you can look at these but first of all, man is to be the provider. You'll notice it says in Genesis 2:15, "The LORD God took the man and put him in the garden of Eden to work it and keep it." Notice that work began before the fall. It is good to work. Work is not the product of sin entering into the world. Already then God made us to work, and man was to keep the garden and to till it. "And the LORD God commanded the man, saying, 'You may surely eat of every tree of the garden,'" but there's one tree you should not eat from (Genesis 2:16–17). Man had the responsibility of making sure there would be food to eat. He was to be the provider.

On the other side, the woman was to be the nurturer. She was to nurture life, and you can see this in femininity and masculinity, can't you? Somehow, the heart of a woman, if she has children, is with those children all the time. She will think about the needs of her children, the needs of her grandchildren, well above her own needs. She will do this because God has put that into her heart. She will always have a sensitive spirit, and not only for human beings but also for animals. You notice this, don't you? There are stories that could be told. You know, a man runs over a squirrel and the squirrel is gasping his last breath, and the wife wants to stop and see whether or not they can do something for it—maybe take it to the ER or something like that. That's part of femininity and masculinity.

The man is to be the provider. He's also supposed to be a leader. Now this is indicated throughout the Scriptures. We don't have time to go into the New Testament where this is even more clearly laid out, but Adam was created first, and in being created first, he had the opportunity of naming the animals over which he was to have control. You'll notice God said, "Adam, you are in charge of nature and you can control nature." If you can name them, you can control them. So Adam had that responsibility as a leader.

She is to be a helper—a helpmeet for him. Many people have looked at this and they've forgotten [that] this is in no way speaking against or belittling the role of a woman. When it says she is to be a helper, the same Hebrew word is used for God. God is our helper and the woman is to be the helper of the man. So she has this responsibility, and as we indicated, she will strengthen and nurture and encourage and receive that which is appropriate from the man. She is to be the helper.

He is also supposed to be the protector. That is, the man is to protect the woman, and this becomes clear in the New Testament as well. As a matter of fact, the Bible says we have a responsibility to our wives, and that will be looked at more specifically in another message in this series. Notice in Genesis 3, where the fall occurred—here is Adam having the responsibility of protecting his wife and he doesn't. Passive Adam. Where did the passivity of men begin? It began even before the fall. Look at what the text says. Genesis 3:6 says, "So when the woman saw that the tree was good for food, and that it was a delight to the eyes, and that the tree was to be desired to make one wise, she took of its fruit and ate, and she also gave some to her husband who was with her, and he ate."

Adam, what in the world are you doing there, standing right next to your wife, knowing that God gave a command that [the fruit from] this tree was not to be eaten? It was forbidden. You stood there and you watched it happen. I think maybe the first sin wasn't Eve eating the fruit. It was Adam standing there, letting her do it without telling her this should not be done in accordance with God's command.

So, Adam is to be the leader. He's always going to struggle with leadership. She is going to be the companion, and of course, after the fall especially, things are set up for some strife. Where God is speaking, He speaks to Eve and says, "I will surely multiply pain in childbearing; in pain you shall bring forth children. Your desire shall be contrary to your husband, but he shall rule over you" (Genesis 3:16). Conflict is built into that verse in the third chapter.

She is also a woman of beauty, as I mentioned. Man has strength and she has beauty. Now I need to say not only are women beautiful, but they also desire to create beauty. A woman doesn't simply move into a house. She weaves her way into that house. All of the knick-knacks have to be in place because she is a lover of beauty. As a result of this, you also have a major difference.

Men are something like a submarine in an ocean, floating around looking for trouble [*laughter*], and if there is no trouble, they create some. Women have sonar. They pick up all kinds of signals that are totally imperceptible to men. Men just don't get it. A woman will say to her husband, "You know, that guy you work for? There's something about him that troubles me." He says, "Well, what is it?" She says, "Well, I don't know what it is. It's just that it's there and he bothers me." And then nine out of ten times, a year later, you realize she was absolutely right. We as men need it said to us, we need it written down with the key words underlined, before we understand something. We don't pick up on anything. No, I'm sorry. We don't notice there is a different picture on the wall than there was when we left in the morning. [*laughter*] And if she has a new hairdo, commend us for recognizing that, but please don't ask us to contrast it to the way it was before she went to the beauty parlor. Don't ask us those questions. We just don't get it and they think because we don't get it, we don't care. No, I'm sorry, we just don't get it.

Those of you who are not married, you have to understand how things can go badly in just a moment of time in a marriage relationship. Things can be sailing along very smoothly and then, in a few moments, it can all come unraveled. In a book on marriage, I read the story of a man who was coming home for his tenth wedding anniversary. He stopped to buy a beautiful card with a very beautiful message. He took time to write something very beautiful in it. His wife is anticipating a wonderful evening; she has a meal planned. He is anticipating a wonderful evening. He is so proud of himself when he walks through the door and hands her the card he has just purchased with all these wonderful things on it, and everything is just sweet. She looks at it and she notices it is not an anniversary card. It is a birthday card. [*laughter*] They end up having their anniversary dinner in separate rooms.

I'm sorry, ladies. I heard an "amen" back there. I don't know who that was. [*laughter*] What are the implications of all of this? How does this all translate?

Number one, please keep in mind that together, man and woman are to mirror the image of God, and to represent the Trinity. This is a larger discussion we can't get into, but notice in Genesis 1:26 it says, "Then God said, 'Let us make man in our image, after our likeness. And let them have dominion over the fish of the sea and over the birds of the heavens and over the livestock and over all the earth and over every creeping thing that creeps on the earth.'" Adam is to rule and Eve is to rule with him as a co-ruler. God created her in the image of God, and He created Adam in the image of God, and when they are brought together, they represent the image of God in a unique way.

Now if you're here and you are single, of course you are created in the image of God. Of course you can represent the image of God, but there is a uniqueness to the marriage relationship, where a man and woman are brought together. They are equal but different with different roles and different responsibilities, and they are brought together with a sense of harmony and with a unity that is actually found in the Trinity. Perhaps later I'll explain that to you in another message.

Second, please notice (and now it's time for mama's boy to look into the text) Genesis 2:24 says, "Therefore a man shall leave his father and his mother and hold fast," the older translations say *cleave*, "to his wife, and they shall become one flesh." When it talks about leaving, it speaks to the man. Why? It's because if a man is strong and knows what he wants in life, his wife is going to follow him. The bigger problem may be a man's relationship to his father and his mother rather than his wife's relationship to them, though that can become a problem, too. It is time for the mama's boy, who I told you about at the beginning of this message, to sit down with his mother and draw some boundaries, and say, "Mother, I love you. Thank you for raising me." Remember, the bonding took place because she probably needed her boy just as much as he needed her because she didn't have a husband. He needs to sit down and say, "These are the boundaries. Here are the rules."

Men, if you don't have clear boundaries regarding your relatives and your in-laws and your parents, your wife will never believe you really treasure her in your heart, and if a wife feels she is not treasured, she will be unfulfilled.

Key words in this passage: you *leave* father and mother, you *cleave*, and then you *become*. And that's what God is asking us to do in our marriages, and we can't do this on our own, can we? This is why God has called us to Himself and to know that ultimately, as we come together, what a means God uses to show us our sinfulness. Remember, marriage is something like holding up a mirror and seeing yourself for what you are in all of your sinfulness and all of your need.

And finally, please keep in mind the whole purpose of marriage is to represent the relationship of Jesus Christ and the church. Many people, when they come to Ephesians 5, they say to themselves, "You know, Paul was looking for a good analogy of Jesus Christ and the church, so what he did was he looked around and said 'You know, I think marriage is a great example of it.'" No, that's not it at all. The whole purpose of marriage is so that God might have an illustration of the relationship between Jesus Christ and the church—Jesus Christ, having died for us and having given Himself for us.

I know this is tough news. It's tough news for me and it's tough news for you as a married man, but we are to be Jesus Christ to our wives, and our wives are to be the church to us, and the implications of that are unbelievable and awesome.

You say, "Well, I'm married to a man, and he has no interest in Jesus Christ or religion and all of that." God still holds him responsible for that because that's what the imagery is really all about. And remember this, when we sin, Jesus doesn't sin in return. When we feel our mate sins against us, this is not a time for us to sin against them. It is a time for us to step back and to ask what patience, love, understanding, and forgiveness is God teaching me as a result of this relationship, despite my disappointment or despite my pain.

In a few moments we're going to remember what Jesus Christ did for us, and the blood that was shed, and the body that was broken on our behalf. And that's what marriage is all about. It's about giving ourselves to others—to someone else—and they giving themselves to us selflessly, caring about one another and representing the gospel to a very, very broken world.

If you are here today and you've never taken advantage of what Jesus Christ has done for us, remember this. He died on the cross to purchase the church, and if you trust Christ, you can be a part of that, and your marriage, hopefully, will represent that glorious relationship.

Let's pray.

Father, we do ask in the name of Jesus that you might help us to understand—to understand our mates, to have a biblical point of view and, above all, to represent you in a broken world. Bless the thoughts we have given, and particularly for those who have never trusted Christ as Savior, may they believe and be saved. We pray this in Jesus' name, Amen.

SERMON FOUR

THE PUZZLE OF THE WILL OF GOD

We're so glad you have joined us today as we continue this series on the topic of marriage, specifically, *The Marriage Puzzle*, and it is a puzzle. In this series of messages, we're trying to put some pieces together.

Today's message is a little different even though it is part of the series. It's entitled, "The Puzzle of the Will of God." The reason I've decided to speak about that is because, when you stop to think of it, there are many couples who wrestle with whether or not they should have been married at all. Have you ever noticed there are some people who go from one destructive relationship to another? If you begin to analyze why, there are many different reasons, but one question I have sometimes asked couples who haven't married well (they have married badly, shall we say) is: "Did you really seek God about your marriage and about your wedding?" Oftentimes they say, "No, we just simply assumed we were both Christians and it seemed reasonable."

My friend, when it comes to momentous decisions, and marriage certainly is the most momentous decision next to whether or not you'll be a Christian, it is not enough to say, "Well, yeah, we kind of did." And that's why we're talking about the will of God.

In some instances, it's very clear as to why the marriage didn't work out. I remember a young woman whom I shall call Ruth who was involved with a man. She was warned to not marry Dan because Dan had a host of problems. She said, "I've seen him at his worst, and I can endure it." So she negated all of the good advice she was given, and we should not be surprised that they were divorced perhaps two or three months later. Many stories like that could be told, but I am talking today about those who say, "Yeah, we did ask

God's blessing on our marriage," and yet in retrospect you question whether they were really following God's lead.

Today's message isn't so much a sermon as it is you and me sitting down for a cup of tea, and I'm looking into your eyes, and we're talking about the will of God. This message is directed to those of you who are not married who think, at some point, you might be or you are seeking God's will in any other aspect—your vocation, your education. All of that is going to be involved in the principles I am going to be giving you in a moment. Or maybe you are in a marriage and you say, "What is God's will within this situation?" I hope that becomes clear as well.

You know, James 1:5 says, "If any of you lacks wisdom, let him ask God, who gives generously to all without reproach, and it will be given him." There is no way I could possibly count the number of times I claimed that verse. Sometimes [when] I have been on the telephone, people have asked me a question, and I haven't known how to answer and I just shoot up a prayer to God—James 1:5, "Lord give me wisdom because, at this moment, I don't have any." Sometimes after I pray that prayer, I wish my conversation had been recorded because I come up with good stuff. [*laughter*] It's too bad it is lost—all attributed to the grace of God.

So with that introduction, let's bow for prayer, because I want you to ask for wisdom regarding the decisions you make, and that God would guide us. Please join me.

Father, in these moments, we ask you to give us wisdom. Give me wisdom. I've prepared this message but Lord, only you can direct me. Even as I give it, may it be a message filled with biblical wisdom. And for those, Lord, who are facing decisions about their future, whether it is marriage or other important choices, give them wisdom and help us to be able to accept how you direct us. In Jesus' name we pray, Amen.

Before we get to the seven principles I want to share with you, let me just simply give you a few preliminaries. First of all, I don't think God is reluctant to guide us. I really don't believe God is in heaven saying, "Oh, you sent your application to three schools? You said whichever one you'd be accepted in, you'd go to that school, and now you are accepted in all three. I dare you to choose the right one." God isn't playing games with us. He's not saying, "You know I have a mate for you somewhere, but she's in Philadelphia and you are in Chicago. I dare you to try to get together on this." That's not God. He delights to guide us. In Romans 8 it says, "For all who are led by the Spirit of God are sons of God" (Romans 8:14). I believe God loves to lead us.

Second, I think it is very important to really understand that knowing God's will ultimately boils down to knowing God; and the better you know God, the better you are going to understand His leading and have the assurance of being led. See, there are many people who turn away from God, and they do so for many different reasons. Many do because they think God is only vengeance. Because they have sinned and they've messed up, they don't go back to God. What a huge mistake.

You have to understand that guilt and a mess is not God trying to push us away. They are God's means of trying to embrace us and invite us into a closer relationship. God never rejects someone who comes to Him. He is a welcoming God, thanks to Jesus. You need to know that because we all mess up in one way or another. Then you also have to believe God is good. One of the reasons people go their own way (and we know they do) and do their own thing is because they believe if they really surrendered to Him, I mean seriously laid it out, He might do something that would really rob them of happiness and what is best for them. Like one woman said, "Lord, I know the man I am going to marry is an alcoholic but I also know I can handle him, so you may be opposed to this, but I'll take care of it, Lord." Why does a woman or man say that? It's because, at root, we don't believe God is good. You need to believe, my friend, that God is good, and there's no place better to be than in the middle of His will even if you are in a desert than to be in a land of plenty doing your own thing.

It's all about knowing God. Also, it's important to realize, oftentimes, God guides us in ways that are really not dramatic, and yet we look back and we say, "That was God."

Someday, I'd like to tell you the story of my life. In many ways it is very, very uneventful and uninteresting. If it were written up in a biography, I think I'd have a hard time getting my kids to read it, and yet in other ways, it is absolutely filled with providence. I could tell you about sitting in a high school classroom, refusing to fill out an application to go to a certain Bible school because, contrary to all reason, I was going to go to another one, and how that decision impacted everything. I don't know that I would be living in America today. I certainly don't see how I could have been the pastor of The Moody Church if I had made the wrong choice, and at the time, I had no idea that the choice I was making was that impactful.

Let me give you another example. Some of you know this. The first Sunday Rebecca and I came to The Moody Church was in 1977. I had been the pastor of a Baptist church north of here. They had a farewell service the last Sunday of March of that year. It was the first Sunday we woke up without a church to go to. I wanted to go to a different church. Rebecca said, "Let's go to The Moody Church," because I had come to know Pastor Wiersbe. Don't tell people this, but God often leads me through my wife. All right? [*laughter*] Don't let that out.

So, we came here and parking was as tight as a drum. It was far worse than the parking situation is today. I dropped her off. We only had two children at the time. This is 1977. I dropped them off and said, "I'll meet you in the lobby," because I had to find a parking space. As soon as they got out of the car, right here on LaSalle Street, "I can go to the place; somebody pulled out," and I thought, "My, this is fortunate," and I backed in. I went into the lobby and found Rebecca. Pastor Wiersbe walked past me with his overcoat on. I put my hand on his shoulder. He didn't see me. I saw him, and I said, "Pastor Wiersbe, where are you going? It's only ten minutes before the morning service." He said, "Erwin Lutzer, I am sick. I am on my way home. Will you preach for me this morning?" [*laughter*] I preached at The Moody Church that morning. I stood on this platform. Someday, I'll tell you what I was thinking about when I was here. [*laughter*]

Whole steps of God's providence—just nothing but providence. And that became a link in a chain that eventually led me to become the pastor. Was I conscious of God's leading when I was back there? No. I was thinking, "This is my lucky day." I had no idea that behind it was God, and many decisions I have made have been that way, and you've made them that way too, and God has led you.

Well, folks, I think that's enough chitchat, isn't it? Don't you think it's time we get down to the seven principles? Not all of them might apply directly to you, but for many of you, I am praying this message will just be absolutely what you needed to hear. Wouldn't that be great? And now I'll give you the seven principles quickly, or as quickly as God wills.

Number one, the will of God is more about *being* than *doing*. Character is more important than your vocation. It is who you are, and once you take care of being, God will guide you in those matters that are unrevealed. The only verse I am going to ask you to turn to today is 1 Thessalonians 4:3, and we'll look at it quickly. This message will be filled with Scripture, but largely I will be quoting it since the verses come from various parts of the Bible. First Thessalonians 4:3 says, "This is the will of God." Well, you come and say, "Pastor Lutzer, I don't know God's will." Well, aren't you ever lucky you came to church today if you believe in luck. "For this is the will of God,"—we finally found it—namely, "your sanctification: that you abstain from sexual immorality; that each one of you know how to control his own body in holiness and honor, not in the passion of lust like the Gentiles who do not know God" (1 Thessalonians 4:3–5).

Wow. There's the will of God: that you be morally pure. See, that's why it is that, if you are sleeping with your girlfriend, you'll never be in a position where you'll know you are being led by God. You won't know what to do. You are only going to make a whole series of bad decisions. You don't know whether to get married, and you are going to have trouble making other decisions too. Why? It's because you are disregarding the clear Word of God. This is His will.

David committed murder and adultery, and he hung out for several months, not really willing to deal with it until Nathan, the prophet, came to him. Then in Psalm 32 he [David] said, "Lord, I confess my sin. I was under all this pressure. My conscience was bothering me and I was trying to put it off." He said, "I confessed my sin and my iniquity I didn't hide, and now you have forgiven me." And what does it say in Psalm 32:8? God says to him, "I will instruct you and teach you in the way you should go; I will counsel you with my eye upon you." Sin is confessed. Guidance is back.

You're living in sin, and you have no idea. You can't hear God's voice. Then the next verse says, "Hey, don't be like the horse and the mule. You know they need bridles so they stay close to you and don't run away." Don't be the kind of a Christian that God always has to have a bridle on or a hook to keep bringing you in. Be an obedient Christian and hear His voice." Now, this isn't the only passage in the Bible (in the New Testament) where it says, "This is the will of God." There are others. When you begin to do the will of God in matters that have been revealed, God will begin to lead you in matters that are unrevealed—your vocation or your choice of a mate, etc.

So, first of all, the will of God is more about being than doing.

Secondly, the will of God doesn't mean our decisions are trouble free.

There's no use second-guessing on this point. Jesus said to the disciples, "Get into a boat and go to the other side," and they were in the will of God. Don't you wish you'd hear Jesus that plainly? Wouldn't that be wonderful if you heard the voice of God with that clarity? "Get in the boat and go to the other side." In the middle of doing the will of God, the biggest storm they had ever encountered came upon them. Just because you are seeking God's will and you do God's will in relationship to a mate does not mean your marriage is going to be conflict-free. It's no guarantee that one of you may not become unfaithful. It's no guarantee that you might not run into a lot of problems, and there's no use second-guessing it at this point because blessed is he "who swears to his own hurt and does not change." The point to keep in mind is that the will of God is not trouble-free.

Here's a couple that makes a decision to buy a house. This is a true story. They pray about it. They give it to God. God leads them. The money is provided for, and after they move in, they discover that the value of the house falls. It has more problems than they realized. It is a money pit, and now they are beginning to ask if they were led by God or they weren't. Well, didn't you give the decision to God? Didn't you submit it all to God and say, "God, whatever your will is, that's what we want"? Yes, we did that. Who is to say then that you weren't led by God? Listen, there are lessons maybe that old rickety houses will teach you that nothing else will teach you. It doesn't mean you are out of God's will. God's will is often really, really filled with trouble.

Third, and this highlights it, the will of God supersedes our personal happiness. Mark that down. Write it in your Bible. Don't forget it. It supersedes personal happiness. In Matthew 26:39 Jesus said, "My Father, if it be possible, let this cup pass from me." And then He said those memorable words that we all know by memory, "Nevertheless, not as I will, but as you will." Was Jesus in the will of God when He went to the cross? The answer, of course, thankfully, is yes. What He said was, "It is not my will but yours." Are you willing to say that in relationship to marriage? I'm speaking now to you singles. Are you willing to say, in relationship to the mate you are dating, "Not my will, Lord, but your will. Whatever it is that you want, that's what I want"? Are you willing to say that?

You see, whenever there is trouble in our lives, the first thing we ask is, where's the escape hatch? Where is the divorce lawyer? How can I get out of this pain? Well, there's another question we should try to ask and that is:

"How do I bring glory to God in the midst of my predicament?" The answer to those questions might not be the same. How do we bring glory to God in the midst of our need because it supersedes personal happiness? God isn't into saying, "Now, you know I am committed to your happiness."

I remember a woman saying to me, "I want out of this marriage because I can't believe God would want me to be unhappy." Lady, what if Jesus had said that in Gethsemane? "I can't believe the Father wants me to go through this pain. Let me go back to heaven and leave the world unredeemed." The will of God sometimes is very difficult. Rebecca and I know a couple that have worked as missionaries and they had to send their children to a school far away. Those children missed their mommy and daddy so much, and before they left, their daughter, who perhaps was (I don't know) eight or ten years old, said, "Mommy, why does Jesus ask us to do such hard things?" Sometimes, Jesus asks us to do very hard things. So, the will of God supersedes our personal happiness. It is God's will and not ours that is the big issue.

Number four, God's will can be communicated in various ways. You say, "Well, how does He guide us?" There are various ways that He guides us. For example, it says in Proverbs 11:14, "In an abundance of counselors there is safety." One way God guides us if you are facing an important decision is [to] get with someone who has some wisdom and ask their opinion, or ask the opinion of a group of people whose opinions you can trust. Nowhere is this more important than in the business of finding a mate. Love is blind, but believe me, the neighbors aren't, and if you have a good family, your family isn't. Take their advice. So, one way is the multitude of counselors. The other is Acts 16 where Paul says, "We wanted to go to this certain place to preach but the Holy Spirit prevented us" (see also Acts 16:6–7). How did the Spirit prevent them? I'm not sure, but I know this. The Holy Spirit has prevented me from some terrible, terrible decisions.

When I was in seminary, I met a young woman whom I shall call Anna. If you were to look at the way in which we met and all of the circumstances, there was absolutely no doubt in my mind that this was a match made in heaven. I mean, really! I won't go into the details except to say that nobody could have put the pieces of this puzzle together except God, so that seemed to indicate that it was God's will. That's what really threw me off, the circumstances. Furthermore, we really loved each other. That was a second component that was important. But there was something else, and that was this business of personal peace. The Spirit of God leads those who belong to God, and something happened within me as we got to know each other that brought me such deep depression and agony. I'm being very vulnerable here today, but it was like two rivers within me, one wanting to go this way and one wanting to go that way. I could hardly live, and yet all of the signs were that, obviously, she was for me. My friends were saying, "Well, look at the way God brought you together," and on and on and on. But within my soul, there was this anguish. Finally, let me make a very long story short—a story that should be short but turned out to be long because, you know, it takes God a long time for God to get through to some of us. It's like the farmer who said, "The way to get a mule's attention is, first of all, to hit him over the head with a two-by-four."

I said to God one evening, "If you are not in this, throw a brick at me." In the morning I was so depressed, I couldn't get out of bed—and I got the message. Folks, if I had married that woman, subsequently knowing the way things turned out for her, I probably would not be in the ministry today.

There are a couple of lessons here for you young people. It's possible to be madly in love with someone who you should not marry. Remember that. Another lesson is the peace of God should rule in your heart. There was a check in my spirit, a huge check, and I look back at that time with deep gratitude to God and say, "God, how could you be this good to me to have spared me?" I don't know why God doesn't spare other people. He had another young woman in mind for me whose name was Rebecca—the right one.

Folks, God communicates His will in various ways. Don't tell me just because you happen to meet at an airport in Seattle and you get along so well and you fall madly in love that that's a basis for finding the right one, unless there are some other things in place.

Number five, doing the will of God is not doubt-free. It's not doubt-free. It's not as if we can say all of our decisions can be made with one hundred percent certainty. I wish that were true, but that's not been my experience. I don't know about you, but in 2 Corinthians 1, the church was criticizing Paul because he planned to come and then he changed his mind. And they were saying, "Does this mean that you are vacillating? First of all it's yes, and then it's no, and so forth." Paul is defending himself and saying, "When it comes to Jesus, it's not yes and no. It's only yes" (see 2 Corinthians 1:15–19). What he's saying is that the important thing is the gospel is to be preached.

But here's the mighty apostle Paul changing his mind because he's not sure exactly what the mind of God is. Oftentimes, we walk with God and we have to make decisions. I mean, you know you can't endlessly sit on an opportunity to leave Chicago and go to Atlanta. They give you two weeks to decide. You can't do that forever. You have to decide, and sometimes we make a decision with trepidation and misgivings; but as we submit it to God, we do that trusting God. And my experience has been that after we make a decision like that, then God begins to confirm it in this way and that way, and we look back and say, "I wonder why I agonized so much over this, because it's so clear that this is what I should have done."

A number of years ago, I was walking through the forest preserve near our condo with little Samuel, our grandson. We actually have three grandsons, and I was walking with him when he was about five, and we took a trail. Then we were coming back and I said, "Samuel, we have to go on this trail." My grandchildren call me Papa and he said, "No, Papa, no, Papa, we have to take this trail," and he was off by about eighty-five or ninety degrees. He would have gone to a river, actually. I knew that forest preserve. I've walked in it a hundred times. I could even see the top of our condo above the trees. "No, Papa." I said, "Samuel, you have to trust," and he said, "Yeah, Papa, but it is so hard to trust," and then he walked behind me kicking leaves as he went. Was he confident this was going to end up right? No, he had some misgivings, but after we turned the corner and saw the condo, I'm sure he thought, "Well, Papa's right."

Listen, my friend, God knows all the trails in the forest preserves. He can see around corners. You know what? It's hard to trust, but that is the best policy. I'd rather trust Somebody who can see the future. We should always trust Him.

Number six, the will of God is often found not by walking so quickly, but rather by waiting. This one needs explanation because it says, "They who wait for the Lord, their sole expectation is from you." "I wait before the Lord," the psalmist says over and over again. Now, don't misunderstand. When I say we should wait before God, I do not mean passivity. J.I. Packer tells the story of a woman he knew who never got out of bed until she felt led of the Holy Spirit to do so. Then after she got out of bed, she needed to feel led before she put her socks and shoes on. That's just silliness. That's not what it means to wait on God. Some of you are maybe looking for employment and you've got no résumés out there. You've got nothing going on. All you are doing is saying, "I'm waiting on God," which is another way of saying, "I'm doing nothing." That's not what the psalmist means. What the psalmist means is you are waiting on God with a sense of expectation, a willing obedience. You are not manipulating. You are not panicking, but you are waiting, and you are working while you are waiting. And you are investigating while you are waiting because what you want to do is to walk with God, and you are trusting Him to guide you. Eager dependence on God.

Number seven—oh, this is such good news. Could you handle a little good news today? You know, you watch television and it's all bad news. Well, here's good news: The will of God encompasses our mistakes and our regrets. It encompasses it. God is adequate for it. You look at the past and you say, "Well, you know I got off the trail." Like the old saying goes, "When you come to a fork in the road, take it." So you say, "I made these wrong decisions, and one wrong decision led to another, and that led to another, and that took me to a part of my life where I didn't want to go, but I was in a box, etc." Listen, God is bigger than all of that.

Joshua does not ask the counsel of the Lord. He doesn't pray about his decision with the Gibeonites, and believes their story. Then they are stuck with the Gibeonites because, "Blessed is he who swears to his own hurt but doesn't change." So, Joshua is stuck with the Gibeonites. Does God say, "Well, that's it; I'm pretty well through with you; you didn't ask my counsel so go ahead and live with it?" Yeah, God says that maybe, but then He says something else. He says, "I'll make the Gibeonites a blessing to you," and they were hewers of wood and carriers of water, and then they ended up going back and helping build the temple.

You know, there's Adam and Eve in the garden. Is there any chance Adam married the wrong one? [*laughter*] Notice this. He did blame her even though he didn't have that chance. You know, Adam says to the Lord, "The woman thou gavest me—if you had led me a little better God, I wouldn't be in this mess." So you know, they mess up, right? In paradise. They mess up. And what does God say in Genesis 3:15? He says these words to the serpent, "I will put enmity between you and the woman, and between your offspring and her offspring; he shall bruise your head, and you shall bruise his heel." It's a contrast of wounds. It's the first prediction in the Bible that Jesus was coming.

Jesus was going to come in the middle of a world broken with sin, broken with stupid decisions and foolishness, and Jesus was going to come and straighten that out, and He still straightens it out because God is a redeeming God.

True story. Nice Christian girl meets boy in Christian school. They get along very well. They take a long trip so she can introduce him to her family. They are on the way back and it's getting late and they decide to spend the night, and of course they don't have much money, and so his intention is that they stay in the same room. There's a check in her spirit that says, "This isn't right." What she should have done is to holler and say, "No, you go ahead and use the room. I'll spend the night in the car." But many women do not have the power—we need to empower them—to make those right decisions for reasons that will become clearer in a future message. So, they spend the night together. Later on, he confesses the reason he did it. He said, "I knew that if you slept with me you wouldn't say no to me when I asked you to marry me." And that's right. You have a relationship like that, and the person you have a relationship with has power over you. It's called a soul tie. It's huge. It'll either end in anger or end badly in other ways. It's inevitable.

But anyway, she now feels an obligation to get married, so she wrote me a long letter telling me this story. Later on, I met the couple, and she is planning her wedding with shame and regret. Isn't that awful? A day that is supposed to be a day of happiness. She said she was like a robot. She was just doing what needed to be done, putting all of her emotions on hold.

Well, they had a few rough years of marriage for various reasons, but I'm telling you this story because it has a happy ending. They are in Christian work today, and they are serving the Lord in a very responsible position, and after she gave me the letter and I read it, I contacted her and said I'd like to meet your husband. I'd like to see this guy you married back then, with your marriage having begun so badly. It was great to see them, and it was great to see that they are happy, that they have children, and God is using them mightily. Why? It is because God is a redeeming God. Aren't you glad He is? He's a redeeming God. I think you ought to clap there if you're awake. [*applause*] If He weren't, where would we be?

If you are here today (and I don't know what your need is), or if you are listening by whatever means, the fact is, God is a redeeming God. Would you come to Him? Would you finally get dead honest? Would you say, "Not my will but yours be done?" And would you trust Him, not when the mess gets better, but in the middle of your mess and your decision-making, and trust Him all the way home?

Let's pray.

Father, guide us in all of our decision-making, we ask. Guide those who are unmarried. Guide those who are married. Help us to seek your will alone, and may we say from the bottom of our hearts, "All for Jesus." We want to give it all to you today. Help us to give it up and to trust you alone. In Jesus' name we pray, Amen.

SERMON FIVE

THE PUZZLE OF YOUR NEEDS AND CONFLICTS

There is a story about two men in a cemetery, and one was overhearing as the other was standing at a grave. The man at the grave kept saying, "How could you do that to me? How could you do that? Why did you die? Why did you die?" So as they were about to leave, they fell in step and the one said to the other, "You know, I just want to give to you my condolences because I heard you say, 'Why did you die? How could you do that to me?' I'm sure that was the grave of your wife." He said, "No, that was the grave of my wife's first husband." [*laughter*]

Why is it that marriage that has such great potential for good things can sometimes go badly? We should not be surprised there is conflict in marriage. A couple hundred years ago, Richard Baxter said this to men about marriage: "Remember still that you are both diseased persons, full of infirmities; and therefore expect the fruit of those infirmities in each other; and make not a strange matter of it, as if you had never known of it before. If you had married one that is lame, would you be angry with her for limping? Or if you had married one that had a putrid ulcer, would you fall out with her because it stinketh? Did you not know beforehand, that you married a person of such weakness, as would wield you some matter of daily trial and offense? If you could not bear this, you should not have married her; if you resolved that you could bear it then, you are obligated to bear it now. Resolve therefore to bear with one another; as remembering that you took one another as sinful, frail, imperfect, persons, not angels, or as blameless and perfect." Well, he says, "You can't take two sinners, self-willed, with different backgrounds, throw them together, and then expect complete and total harmony all the rest of your life. Realize that conflict is part of marriage."

Speaking of that, I have two true stories for you very briefly. Both are ones I know about. The wife speaking to me about her husband says, "He's so oppressive that sometimes I think I am in a concentration camp in Auschwitz, yet he expects me to make love with him. I feel as if it would be like a guard coming to a woman in a concentration camp for intimacy and expecting her to enjoy it."

Here's another one from a husband: "The minute my wife comes home, she is on the internet. If she does cook, it's just warming up some food she bought in a store. Then beginning about 7:00 p.m., she goes upstairs to her computer and is on a social website until about 11:00 p.m. She has a group of friends she connects with. These friends are obviously more important than I am, so we live in the same house, receive mail at the same address, but that's about all. What makes this doubly bad is that I am a pastor and she works as a counselor in a Christian counseling center."

Well, I'm going to have something to say to both of these couples before this message is over. Let me say that the purpose of this message is to discuss the needs we all have. It is to discuss conflicts. We're going to look at conflict and we're going to take it apart. We're going to get at the essence of conflict. We're going to look beyond the superficial and get to the heart of it. It's going to be like hitting a piñata at a Mexican festival. Suddenly, it's all going to come together and we're going to find out what in the world is inside of this business of conflict. Why are there so many arguments that are never resolved? Today, you are going to find out why. The other purpose of this message is to give us a way out, to give us a way of ending arguments, of understanding one another, and living happily after.

Do you think one message can do all of that? You know, I don't think so, because there are some of you who are going to listen to this message and you're going to say, "I finally got it; now I understand why we can never get on the same page." And there are some of you who will not get it, because no matter how much truth, it's going to be like bullets off Batman's chest. It's just not going to penetrate. And though what I have to say is so incredibly important, and for some of you, your marriage might be at stake, my message can't do it. Only God can. I pray He might use this message. Ultimately, only God can do the miracles we're looking forward to today as a result of what I have to share with you.

So, would you bow with me in prayer? No matter by what means you are listening today, I want you to pray right now and say, "God, speak to me. May I get it."

Father, I have the faith to pray that as a result of this message, some homes, where there is only noise, will finally have harmony. And where there's been conflict and arguing that, at last, there will be some peace. Show us, Lord, in our own lives what we lack and show us what we need to do with such clarity and conviction that we don't miss the message. We pray in Jesus' blessed name, Amen.

I need to say that, for the major insight in this message, I'm indebted to a book entitled, *Love and Respect*, by a man by the name of Emerson Eggerichs. One of his insights comes from the fifth chapter of the book of Ephesians, and that, by the way, is our text for today, Ephesians 5. He believes the thing that is of the essence is found in Ephesians 5:33. It says, "However, let each one of you (speaking to husbands) love his wife as himself, and let the wife see that she respects her husband."

Now here's the bottom line. A wife's primary need is to be loved by her husband. She needs to know she is number one in his life and she is cherished and treasured. That's her number one need. The number one need of a man is that he might be respected. If he's not respected, he is not having a fundamental God-given need met. Think about this for a moment. What happens is this: What does a wife do if she doesn't feel loved? If she doesn't feel loved, she lashes out in a way that is very disrespectful, so all he has coming to him is this disrespect. Now that he is receiving disrespect, how is he going to react to this disrespect except to come across as very unloving. So, you have two people arguing. Their basic needs are not met and the more they argue, and the more they disagree, the more their fundamental needs are not being met, and so Eggerichs calls this "the crazy cycle" that goes on year after year after year with nobody having their fundamental needs met, and nobody understanding why they can't get on the same page and why they can't stop their arguing.

She's saying, "Love me and treasure me, and I promise you I'll be different." He's saying, "Respect me and I will treat you differently," and neither of them are giving each other what they need.

Now if that were the whole story, it would be bad enough, but it's worse than that because, you know, there are men who maybe love their wives, but the wife doesn't feel as if she is loved, so what's this guy supposed to do? And there may be wives who respect their husbands, but the husband feels no respect. You see how difficult this becomes? Add to that the fact that we see our own faults very differently than we see the faults of other people. We magnify their faults and we [can only] see ours under a microscope, it's so small.

Maybe now we can begin to understand why General MacArthur used to tell the troops at West Point, "Gentlemen, don't even think of getting married until you've mastered the art of warfare." [*laughter*] We now get it, don't we?

What we're going to do is to look at the Bible and see what love is and find out what respect is, and see whether or not, at last, we can put an end to all these crazy arguments that never end, and we can all get on the same page. Are you with me so far? How many are with me? Can I see your hands please? I'll go with forty percent. [*laughter*]

First of all, what are the needs of a wife? I am picking it up in Ephesians 5:22: "Wives, submit to your own husbands, as to the Lord. For the husband is the head of the wife even as Christ is the head of the church, his body, and is himself its Savior. Now as the church submits to Christ, so also wives should submit in everything to their husbands" (Ephesians 5:22-24).

The fundamental need a wife desires is that her husband lead so she can follow. Some of you wives read this passage of Scripture and already jitters are going through your body. You are full of fear. You are saying, "What do you mean submit? If I were to submit—am I supposed to be a doormat? He's going to misuse me. He's going to mistreat me. He's going to even abuse me."

By the way, that word *abuse* is a heavy-laden term, and that's why the last message in this series on marriage is going to be on abuse. But most of you aren't in that category. What you are simply saying is, "I don't like the fact that I have to be under his authority," and it's because you don't trust God. That's what it says in 1 Peter 3:5. It says the ancient women hoped in God and then they were submissive because they were trusting God. You are taking a risk, to be sure, but the fact is, if you do not respect your husband, and if you are not under his authority, you are going to have conflict in marriage. That's just the way it is.

Now, I do need to clarify, when we talk about submission, it doesn't mean you agree with your husband about everything. Obviously, you won't. It doesn't mean you are going to stop thinking on your own and become a robot and stand in the middle of the room and watch him bark out orders and tell you what to do next. That's not what we're talking about. It doesn't even mean you shouldn't try to change your husband's mind if he has crazy ideas. I think, for example, of Rebecca. She has saved me from an awful lot of stupid decisions. I wouldn't make a major decision without consulting her and asking her input. So that's not what we are talking about. What we are speaking about is, what John Piper likes to say, a disposition on your part that you are going to follow while he leads, and grant him that respect. You ask, "Oh, but what if he's out of line?" You don't lecture to him. You don't put him down, but you do entreat him, and you say, "You know, I want to respect you, and I want to follow you, but considering how you are acting over here, it's making it very difficult for me. Is there some way we can resolve this?" [Do this] because the Bible says that wives should submit to their husbands as the church submits to Christ. Take that in faith.

Now, what else does she obviously need? She needs love. "Husbands, love your wives." You knew it was coming up here in the text because now we are in Ephesians 5:25. "Husbands, love your wives, as Christ loved the church and gave himself up for her." That's the analogy. I have performed many weddings here at The Moody Church. As a matter of fact, I could write a book of cartoons of funny things that have happened at weddings. Get six pastors together and you would have enough cartoons to fill a good-sized book. But when the wife is coming down the aisle, standing here to greet her is Jesus Christ. That's what Paul is saying. "Husbands, you are to be Jesus Christ to your wife." Now, how many of you wives would say, "I married Jesus"? I know mine wouldn't, but that's the analogy. We're supposed to be Jesus Christ to our wives and love her as Christ loved the church.

We say, "Well, how can we do that?" Think about Jesus Christ's love for the church for just a moment. Does Jesus listen to you? Have you ever prayed and Jesus said in effect, "Look, I don't have time to listen to you now…there are huge world events going on, and I'm preoccupied"? No, Jesus listens to you. Gentlemen, there are some things I am going to share directly from my heart to you, and the ladies don't even have to listen if they don't want to. It's for you. Our wives need communication. It's happened a hundred times in our home. Rebecca will tell me something and, two minutes later, I'm asking her about it. Clearly, I wasn't listening. Our wives need to talk and we need to listen, and if you ever become impatient listening, ask yourself, "Does Jesus become impatient and say, 'Hey, you've prayed long enough; I've got other things to do'?"

The other thing is servant leadership. The Bible says that Jesus gave Himself up. You have so many men who say, "Oh, you know, I'm willing to die for my wife." Well, I hope you are. I hope I am, but you know that's not where most of our wives are. My wife is wondering why I don't see that the garbage needs to be carried out; "Start there and then talk about dying for me further down the road." [*laughter*]

Gentlemen, listen. Ladies, you don't have to listen, but you can if you want. Let us suppose you had a plant in your room or in your house—a real plant, not artificial but real—and you walk by it and you notice that it's got all of these brown leaves and it's shriveled up and it's not looking very good. As you leave, you say, "Look at these brown leaves," and you throw them in the air, and you say, "You know, I am so sick of looking at that plant. It doesn't look very good. I think it's time for me to get a new one." It's called divorce. "Let me have somebody who still has some vibrancy. Let me find a plant with some green leaves and with some fruit on it, and none of this dead stuff. I'm in a dead marriage." That's one response. The other response is to say, "Hmm, brown leaves. I'd like to do an analysis of the soil. Let's study the soil in which it grows and let's make sure the plant has water. I know how much to water it, and when to water it, and also let's make sure it has fertilizer, and let's see whether or not this shriveled plant can't begin to grow and to have green leaves again."

I'm giving you reality in this message, all right? Men, we are the soil in which our wives grow, and if we want to have a vibrant wife, if we want to have her satisfied (and my dear friend, put this up as a banner and use it as a bumper sticker, "happy wife, happy life." All right?), [*laughter*] what we need to do is we need to understand her and her needs, because we are the soil in which she grows. Jesus is the soil in which we grow and He gave Himself up for the church. That is really love.

We have to protect our wives. In one of the books I was reading, a couple was going through a museum. They were looking at a Rembrandt painting and, of course, you're not supposed to touch paintings when you are in a museum, and their little child was reaching up to touch the painting and the mother said, "Don't you dare touch that. That's Rembrandt." My dear friend, if you don't touch a Rembrandt painting because you are honoring it, why do you allow anyone or anything to touch your wife who is created in the image of God? She is heir with you of the hope of promise. She is the one you swore to love. It is our responsibility to protect our wives, and then the Bible says to cleanse her "by the washing of water with the word." Men, you should take the initiative to pray with your wife. Well, you say, "I'm not very good at prayer." Most of us aren't, but your wife will appreciate the fact that you are taking that initiative. You are the spiritual leader and if you aren't, learn to be in small ways, and God will bless you and enable you to lead her in bigger ways as time goes on.

And then again, we have to do something Jesus never has to do. He never has to ask for forgiveness and say, "I'm sorry," but we do, and we need to do it often. I think Rebecca will testify that, in our marriage, one of the things I have tried to do, no matter how upset I might be about something, I always like to be quick to say, "Look, I'm sorry. I messed up. Will you forgive me?" I don't see any possibility for a happy marriage without that. That's why, in the Minneapolis–St. Paul airport, a woman came and sat next to us and said, "You must have been married for many years," because she had seen Rebecca buy something I like to eat, and we're sitting there in harmony eating. We said, "Yes." And then she said, "I'm going to get married." Remember me telling that story? And then she said, "What word of advice would you give to someone who has never been married before?" and Rebecca, just as quick as that, Rebecca, as I was rolling my eyes and thinking about where in the world this was going, said, "Learn to forgive." And I thought, "Well Rebecca, now you should turn to me and thank me for the many times [*laughter*] you have been able to practice that particular virtue considering the man you married." A wife's primary need is to be led and to be loved.

What about the husband? Well, "See that she respects her husband," it says in Ephesians 5:33. What that means, when you add to that the whole issue of submission of the wife, is husbands need someone who is reliable and whom they know is dependable. She's not the kind of woman who is spending money behind his back and doctoring the checkbook to cover it up. She's not the kind of person who is conniving. And by the way, speaking of money, it is so huge that the next message in this series has to do with money, because there are so many conflicts over that and so many divorces over that, and that's why we are going to deal with it in the next message in this series on marriage. But "the heart of her husband," the Bible says in Proverbs 31:11, "doth safely trust in her" (KJV). I know God has given me a wonderful wife, and among many, many other virtues, I can say of Rebecca, "My heart does safely trust in her." A man desires that. She's not running off telling other people about how bad he is. She's not the kind of person who is speaking behind his back. He can trust her.

And then, of course, respect. Now, ladies, it's your turn. You respect by the tone of your voice. You can say the right thing, but you can do it in the wrong way, and that can indicate huge volumes of disrespect to your husband. Now here's what women generally think. What if a man were to say to his wife, "Well, you have to earn my love"? Could you imagine saying that as a Christian? She'd say, "Earn your love? Don't you read your Bible? You are supposed to love me unconditionally like Jesus Christ loved the church, and now you are talking to me about earning your love?"

What if he were to say to her, "You have to respect me unconditionally"? She would say, "What do you mean, respect you unconditionally? You have to earn respect." Women sometimes say, "That rat has to earn my respect," so she doesn't respect her husband because, you see, it is conditional and, of course, he never reaches the point where he is worthy of respect—you can be pretty well sure of that—[so] his needs are never met. He acts in an unloving way; her need for love is unmet, and on and on the crazy cycle goes.

One way you can respect him is by the way in which you entreat him. Don't lecture him. If you find out he is struggling with pornography, you don't give him a lecture and shame him. What you do is you say, "I just want you to know how much you deeply hurt me by this. I am a crushed woman, but I want to stand with you through this. We want to get to the heart of it. I want to pray with you and I want to encourage you out of this." By the way, one of the messages still to be preached in this series is on addiction. But she is there to stand with him, to love him, and as best she can, to continue to respect him, even though he so deeply disappointed her.

Ladies, you could change your marriage if you encouraged your husband. Find something you can encourage him in, something you appreciate, something that's good, because it's there. Maybe you have to do a little bit of archeological work to find it. Whole marriages could be changed by the way in which couples speak to one another and by the way in which they engage each other and speak of one another.

You know, I am always reminded of that mother whose daughter came home with her boyfriend and after they left, somebody said to the mother, "Well, what did you think of your daughter's boyfriend?" Trying to think of something positive, she said, "Well, you know, at least the words on his tattoos were spelled correctly." [*laughter*] I mean, find something good. Put a note of encouragement where he'll find it. Respect him. He needs respect. If he doesn't have that, unfortunately, he's probably going to act in unloving ways. He doesn't have to, but that's the tendency.

Where does this all lead us and why should our lives be changed because we've listened to this message? Every time you hear a message, you should say, "Why should my life be changed as a result of this?" That's the whole purpose of preaching. It's not to give you information. It's to change your life, and the information is intended to do the change with the help of the Holy Spirit.

First of all, number one, would you remember this: Our marriages, as Christians, should not tell lies to the world. You see, God instituted marriage to show the relationship of Christ and the church. That's why Paul says this is such a great mystery. This hadn't been revealed yet in Old Testament times as it is in New Testament times. And when we as Christians have bad marriages, what we are saying is that Jesus and the church don't get along very well—this is the way they fight, and this is the way they argue. We are sending a wrong message about Jesus and the church. We need to repent because the purpose of marriage is to bring glory to God and to illustrate the relationship of Jesus, ladies, whom you married; to the church, men, whom you married. That's the purpose.

Now, let's go back to the two stories I began this message with. Let's go back to the woman who said, "My husband is as oppressive as a guard in Auschwitz. All that he cares about is dragging me into the bedroom." That's essentially what she said. What should happen in that situation? The man, supposedly, is a Christian. What should he do? He should back off, and he should think to himself, "Now, wait a moment. How could my wife feel so unloved that she would think this of me? What have I done or not done in order to give her this sense of being used rather than valued?" That should be his first question. So what he ought to do is to study his wife and study his relationship to her and say, "Wherein is this breakdown because she's acting out like this because she doesn't feel loved, so how can I make her feel loved so she won't speak this way about me?"

She, as a Christian, on the other hand, should say, "You know, I overreacted and I didn't speak well about my husband." By the way, she told me this in his presence during a marriage counseling session, and I think if the truth were known, her comment was a little bit over the top as people sometimes do. She should be entreating him rather than lecturing him and trying to tell him off because she's still to respect him. That's not conditional.

Let's go to the situation in which the wife comes home, makes a quick dinner, then goes up and is on the internet from 7:00 to 11:00 p.m. on a social networking site. What she argues is that her husband is so boring and she has these needs that need to be fulfilled. She says, "I find these needs fulfilled with my internet friends, and that's really where I get my fulfillment." Folks, I want you to imagine this woman as a Christian standing in the presence of Jesus on the judgment seat of Jesus Christ where the Bible says all of us are going to be. Let's imagine it. Jesus is asking her about her relationship in marriage and why she neglected her husband, and why she was on the internet for four hours every night, finding fulfillment apart from her marriage, and apart from Him, by the way. And she says, "Well, Jesus, you know our marriage was boring." Jesus says, "Ah yes, that's right. You know, I realize now that you were supposed to respect your husband and be under his authority, but you're right. I didn't mean it if you married a boring husband. You know, it's nothing that drastic. I mean you certainly had a reason why you wouldn't have had to obey my clear word. That sounds good to me."

Do you know what that woman ought to do? She ought to get on her knees and repent and stay there long enough till the rebellion is out of her heart. Then what she should do is go to her husband and ask his forgiveness. Maybe he is boring, but you know, maybe it's been years since he felt respected and maybe it's been years since she felt loved, and what they need to do is to get on with their relationship and the covenant that they made before God and stop all of these silly excuses for their disobedience. That's what they need to do. Could I be any clearer than that? Is there anyone here who says, "What does He really think about these things?" We need to stop lying about Jesus and His relationship to the church. Our marriages are telling lies.

Second, when sinned against, do not sin. What does the man say? "Well, you know I tried to love her and all I get is this contempt." Normally, what happens when a husband receives contempt from his wife is he responds to it, and that is a huge mistake. The Bible says in the book of Proverbs, "Where there is no wood, the fire goes out, the quarrel ends" (see Proverbs 26:20). If you don't respond, at some point she is going to stop talking, I think. I'm reminded of a little cartoon. A little boy said, "My parents argued all evening but my dad never said a word the whole time." [*laughter*] But she is going to stop at some point— and when I say *she*, it could be *he*. You understand all illustrations I give could be flipped over to the other side. Just let it go— and then when she is finished, say, "I am so sorry you feel so unloved that you have to speak to me like that. Could we work on a lot of deeper things than the superficial arguments?" Where there is no wood, the fire goes out.

What happens in a case like that? The two are arguing, and instead of taking the wood out of the fire and not putting more in, he thinks he can fight this fire with a little bit of gasoline. He thinks, "Here's some gasoline. Oh, you know you're blowing up? So here. Oh, you want that? I'll give you that, too." Where does that leave them? It leaves them destroyed with pieces all over the place to pick up. Most of them will never be picked up. It will kind of be smoothed over. The real issues will not be dealt with. They'll go on and the same thing will happen again and again and again. When sinned against, do not sin.

In the 1700s, there was a Scottish pastor by the name of James Fraser. He was a beloved pastor and the author of a couple of books, and a battered husband. It is unclear how the Presbyterians of that day would allow a man with a disobedient wife to be a pastor, but they did. It is said she never provided him with a sit-down meal at their home. Everyone in his parish knew this. He would have starved to death if the church members had not left him pouches of food by the fencepost when he passed by on his pastoral errands. When he returned home at night, he was not able to be in the same room with his wife because he would get a tongue lashing, so he went to his study, but his wife controlled the coal bin and the oil for the lamp, allowing him no fire to warm himself or oil to light his lamp. If he sat still in the dark, he would nearly freeze and, because of this he walked back and forth from one end of the study to the other in the darkness. And because he did, you see, how would you know, if you were in total darkness, when you got to a wall? Well, he kind of kept his hands out and then turned around and went back to the other wall. After he died, they examined his study and found indentations in the plaster where his hands hit the wall on his nightly beat.

Once when the local Presbyterian pastors were gathered together, a toast was offered for the wives of the pastors. The man offering the toast turned to Fraser and said (I'm sure with a touch of sarcasm), "James, you'll want to offer a toast to your wife as well, I assume." "So I will and so I should," said Fraser, "for my wife has been better to me than all of yours put together." Their mouths dropped. "How so?" they asked. He said, "My wife has driven me to my knees seven times a day, and that's more than any of your wives have done for you." [*laughter*] They were probably so happily married they didn't even have to pray.

When sinned against, learn not to sin and you'll never be more like Jesus—because that's exactly what the Bible says. "Who, when he was reviled, reviled not again." He did not render evil for evil, argument for argument. You win this, but I'm going to win this, and here's a zinger for you as a parting shot. No, He was willing to be sinned against, and yet [He did] not sin.

I think it was Joni Eareckson Tada who spoke about the purpose of suffering. She said, and I'm paraphrasing here, "Suffering is like sheep dogs that nip at our heels to force us to walk the hill of Calvary." For some of you, that kind of suffering is in your marriage, unfortunately. But I believe that through repentance and faith, through dealing with issues, you can get beyond that so you can begin to sing together rather than just make noise. But you know, it needs repentance. It needs humility. It needs brokenness, and that leads me to my last point.

Ultimately, the success of all this is the cross of Jesus Christ, the Bible says, who gave Himself up for us all. He died for the church. Because there are some of you listening to this, and this is pretty foreign to you, and the reason is because you're on the outside looking in, you may not be a part of the "church," as the Bible is using the term here. You may be a church member, to be sure, but the Bible is saying that it is because of our forgiveness we receive because of Jesus—because of that forgiveness [that we are a part of the church]. Imagine how much God has forgiven you. In fact, neither you nor I have a clue as to how much God has forgiven us. He has forgiven many of our sins we aren't even aware of, ones we have committed over and over again that we are aware of, plus a whole lot of other things, and the Bible is saying that God is a reconciling God, and we, having been forgiven, forgive.

If you weren't here for the message I preached entitled, "The Puzzle of Your Past," where I talked about forgiveness, I encourage you to get [the CD and listen to it], because some of you need to deal with whole past issues.

All kinds of baggage from the past that need forgiveness and resolution, but at the end of the day, it is the good news of the gospel that enables us to live together on the same page.

If you've never trusted Christ as Savior, remember this: He died so that we could be forgiven, reconciled to God, and belong to God forever. And the way in which we receive that free gift is through the gift of faith and we simply say, "Jesus, I know I'm a sinner, and I believe on you and I trust you, and I trust you to forgive me. I shall trust you to help me to forgive others." Husbands, you can begin to get on the same page, so that you are free to love your wife so she feels loved; and wives, so that you feel free to respect your husbands, because he needs respect. Then live every day of your life confessing that because of our weaknesses and our sins, we need God every single hour.

Would you join me as we pray?

Father, my suspicion is there are many people who are listening for whom this message was specifically intended, but whether or not it will reach its target, and whether blind eyes are opened and cynical hearts are caused to melt is totally dependent upon your Spirit. We ask, Lord Jesus, that you might do that, because now we're waiting for miracles. We're waiting for the dead to rise and the deaf to hear and the blind to see.

How many of you would say, "Pastor Lutzer, I know today's message was intended for me"? Why don't you raise your hand right there as an indication of the Holy Spirit of God working.

Father, those for whom this message was intended and for those who didn't raise their hand, let them not go until they have met you. In Jesus' name, Amen.

SERMON SIX
THE PUZZLE OF YOUR FINANCES

> "Dug from the mountain-side, washed in the glen,
> Servant am I or master of men?
> Steal me, I curse you;
> Earn me, I bless you;
> Grasp me and hoard me, a fiend shall possess you;
> > Lie for me, die for me;
> > Covet me, take me,
> Angel or devil, I am what you make me!"

Today's topic is money. True story. We shall call them Julie and Tom. [They] lived together before they were married. After all, they wanted to save some money and have house equity. After they get married, they decide they are going to buy a house because both of them have jobs. The get some money from Tom's father for the down payment. They also buy a new car because it has zero percent financing. And later on, Julie gets pregnant and there were some complications in the pregnancy, and she has to quit her job, and now they're on one salary. So, Tom goes and he tries to surreptitiously, without her knowing, get a second mortgage on the house to pay their bills. Julie finds out he was being dishonest and now she's angry because she thinks he is wasteful. He says it's really her fault, because it's the pregnancy that messed everything up. One argument leads to another and eventually they get divorced over the matter of money.

It happens so often.

Why is it that money is such a touchy subject? Why is it the thing that sparks so many arguments? A couple of reasons. First of all, it's because money is the essence of living; that is to say, we need money in order to live, and we do.

One of our sons-in-law works for a building company. He said this past week, a man was laid off from his job. He has five children. What is he going to do? He has a mortgage to pay. He's got groceries [to buy.] The kids have needs. They have all kinds of issues, I'm sure. How is he going to make it? I don't know, but I breathed a prayer that somehow he would.

Many of you are in the very same predicament. Many of you have been searching for work for a year or two and the work hasn't materialized. You've been seeking employment and God hasn't seen fit to give you a job, and you're wondering whether you're going to go home today and find the lights turned out. We have many people in our church who are in that kind of a predicament.

The Bible has much to say about the poor. For example, James says there are those who are poor but are rich in faith, and that's wonderful. Sometimes the poor are rich in faith, most assuredly. But I do have to say, and many of you will testify, that poverty can very easily be overrated. My wife and I saw *Fiddler on the Roof,* I think [it was] thirty-five years ago, and I think it was one of the best movies ever produced. Do you remember how Tevye said, "Well, to be poor is no disgrace, but on the other hand, it's no great honor either." And then when the young man comes and says that money is a curse, I think he walks out of the barn and says, "Oh, God, if money is a curse, smite me with it, and may I never recover." Do you remember that?

I'll tell you something, money is the essence of life in this sense: we need money to live. If you don't want to live on the street, you need money to live. That's why it touches us so very deeply. But there's another reason, and that is because money makes so many promises. It has so much seductive power; it makes all the same promises as God. You've heard me say that before, but it's true. God says, "I will be with you and I will never leave you nor forsake you." Money says, "I'll be with you and I'll never forsake you. I'll be there whether there's healthcare or not. I have enough. I can pay for you. I'll be there in old age so you can live in a nice place in your final days. I'll be there to clothe you. I'll be there to give you all the entertainment you want. Tell me the entertainment and I'll be there to do it for you." And so, money comes along and says, "You want to sin. I can fund it."

Before, I told you about a man, and I have to tell the story again because I shall never forget it. He had a stroke and it debilitated him. At first he was very angry, but years afterwards, I asked him if he had ever thanked God for his stroke and he said, "I thank Him every day for it." That surprised me. He said, "You have to understand. I had the time and I had the money to go deeply into sin, and the stroke prevented me." He said, "I thank God every day for it." Oh, money is seductive.

Wave big money in people's faces and they will just become demons. I remember an attorney telling me a story about how a man willed several millions of dollars to a Christian institution, and then the step-children, not his children, objected and they tried to change the will after he died. They got an unscrupulous attorney who even was disbarred later because of all of the things he had done. And here you have this family now torn apart with lies and deceit and one trick after another because, in their minds, they were saying, "Get it honestly if you can, but if necessary, get it dishonestly, but by all means get it." Money makes demons even out of Christians. It is very seductive.

Now with that background, the intention of this message is to give you some principles about money by which we should live. If you had heard this message years ago, it might have spared you some grief; and if I had preached it years ago, it might have spared me some grief as well, but here we are. At the end of the message, I'm going to be outlining how couples can stop all arguments about money. You never have to have another argument about money again. Isn't that great? Just think you have come here to The Moody Church and today we're going to put it all to rest. Don't you wish? [*laughter*] I'm not quite that naïve.

I do know this: I believe these principles will do that [stop arguments about money], but you have to hear from God or you won't like the principles. Therefore, even though we've prayed several times already, I'm going to ask all of us to pray now. And men, I want you to pray; wives, I want you to pray; singles, I want you to pray. Wherever you are, if you're watching this by way of internet all over the world, let us ask God to speak to us because, if you only hear my words, you won't change. What you need to hear today is the Word of God—and God has to change your heart. Would you join me as we pray?

Father, as we come to this sensitive topic of money, make this a transforming experience. We ask, Lord Jesus, that the light of your Word would shine upon us, and that in shining upon us, we might be changed. We pray, Father, that arguments that have taken place in homes for years might end. And we ask, Lord, that couples will be on the same page in their lives and that the Holy Spirit of God would work mightily. And for those who do not know Christ as Savior, we pray they may understand the gospel. In Jesus' name we ask. Amen.

I want you to take your Bibles today and turn to 1 Timothy 6, where we're going to look at these principles. The reason you should be reading your Bible is, always remember, that it is a talking book. When we read the Bible, we hear the voice of God. Maybe you're like me. You've never heard a voice outside of yourself speaking, although I do believe one time I did, but that's abnormal. The point is when we want to hear what God has to say, we open His Word.

In your pew Bibles, it is page 993. Very quickly, I am going to give you five or six principles and then I am going to get on the issue of some practical wisdom of how you can resolve financial conflicts. That's the agenda.

First of all, you'll notice the principle of honesty. To pick this up, I'm going to read 1 Timothy 6. It's talking about false teachers. It says [starting] in verse 4, "He is puffed up with conceit and understands nothing. He has an unhealthy craving for controversy and for quarrels about words, which produce envy, dissension, slander, evil suspicions, and constant friction among people who are depraved in mind and deprived of the truth," and now notice this, "imagining that godliness is a means of gain" (1 Timothy 6:4–5). Let's read just that far.

This is written to the people who will be in Ephesus. That was probably where Timothy was when he received this letter. In Ephesus, godliness was becoming popular, so some people said, "If godliness is where it's at, then that's where we want to be because we want to make a buck on godliness." And they did it through their false teaching, through charging exorbitant fees for what they were doing, and through deceiving God's people with all these arguments and with all these quarrels because they wanted to make a fast buck.

Principle number one when it comes to money is honesty. These people didn't have it. May you and I have it today as Christians. And I would say this, honesty extends to other issues. When you earn money, earn it honestly. A number of years ago, I was in Hong Kong and I bought a camera lens. I was sent there because I was told this man was a Christian, and so he and I talked and he said, "You know, if I were totally honest, I wouldn't be able to compete with all the businesses along this street." He said, "You know, I also have to have some dishonesty to compete." Well, I sat there, and over a period of five or six minutes, I tried to help him consider trying to do something very unreasonable but very biblical. I said, "Why don't you just trust God? Oh, of course, you have to lower your prices because of competition, but you don't have to tell a client he's getting this kind of quality when, in point of fact, he's getting another kind of quality. That kind of deceit dishonors God. Why don't you just trust God and be honest?" I don't know whether he took my advice.

There must be honesty in terms of how you get it, and honesty in your relationship with your spouse. I read this past week that in about fifty percent of all marriages (that's about half of you) one spouse has a secret the other doesn't know about when it comes to finances. A good example is [about] a man I knew who took $30,000 from their joint retirement account and spent it trying to get rich quick on the internet. Of course, I don't have to tell you, do I, that he lost it all? Now there are two things he did wrong. Number one, he didn't ask his wife. She would've had the good sense to tell him this is crazy. Any good wife would have seen that, and wives have the ability to see through that, and that's what she'd have told him, and he would have been spared the agony. And secondly, he did it without her knowing it.

So, I'm speaking today to couples where usually the man says, "Well, you know, I want to spare my wife of all the reality," and she senses back there: dishonesty, deceit, some little lies, and she doesn't know where it's at. Folks, it's time, if you're married, to take everything that is under the table and put it on the table. And don't you dare make any major expenditure unless both of you are agreed that it's a wise one. That's the principle of honesty.

We must hurry on to the principle of contentment. Notice what it says in 1 Timothy 6:6–8: "But godliness with contentment is great gain, for we brought nothing into the world, and we cannot take anything out of the world. But if we have food and clothing, with these we will be content." Will we? I don't think so. Always remember what is the great enemy of the advertising industry, the one enemy they want to destroy, the one enemy they are fighting against, the one enemy they just absolutely hate is contentment. If you're content with this old car, you aren't going to buy a new one. If you're content with the clothes you're wearing, you aren't going to need to get new ones.

And by the way, I'll throw this in at no extra charge, I think, probably, Eve is one of the only women in the world who said to her husband without lying, "I have nothing to wear." [*laughter*] But you see, today, though we have food and clothes, we are not content. We're discontent. Paul is saying, "If you have the basics, blessed is the person who is content with them." But we aren't content. And then you have the credit card coming along, and the credit card says, "You don't have to be content."

You know, when I was growing up, we weren't dirt poor, but we were poor. I could tell you stories. When we wanted something, we used to have to pray [that] God would somehow get it to us, or somehow we'd get the money to get it. Today, the credit card says, "God, we won't have a thing to do with you. We won't depend upon you. If we need a different car, we'll simply go and we will borrow the money, and we'll use the credit card, and we don't need you anymore."

Those old days about praying about needs—they're gone. Nine thousand three hundred dollars is what the average couple has on their credit card if they're not the kind of people who pay [it off] at the end of the month. And there are a few people who pay at the end of the month, and for them the credit card is great, but they are a minority.

Do you know what else the credit card companies know? They know you will spend at least one-third more with a credit card. Can you imagine taking your family to a restaurant and laying down say seventy or eighty dollars to have a meal together—you and the kids? Are you telling me you'd do that if you didn't have a credit card? Are you telling me you'd actually take out your wallet and you would count out ten, twenty, thirty, forty? There's no way you would do that, but you give them a piece of plastic. Of course I don't think it's wrong to borrow for appreciating items. I know houses have gone down in value, but generally speaking, when you buy something like that, it's going to appreciate. But you buy a new car and make payments, and you drive the thing across the street and it's lost $500. So, what we must do is to recognize the absolute curse of debt. Remember debt, devil, and dirt are all related, and some of you are in debt because you're buying groceries now with credit cards, and I understand that, and that's a need, and I'm going to be talking about getting on the same page a little later on, but the thing is contentment.

Notice what it says about those who aren't content. I'm reading 1 Timothy 6:9–10 now, "But those who desire to be rich fall into temptation, into a snare, into many senseless and harmful desires that plunge people into ruin and destruction. For the love of money is a root of all kinds of evils. It is through this craving that some have wandered away from the faith and pierced themselves with many pangs." Wow. What's that all about?

Listen, if you are covetous, if you are greedy, greed never is content to be alone. Greed will always bring other sins with it—always new explorations, always a new way to assert your power and your value. That is how money can be a curse, because now suddenly it becomes not the root of all evils, but a root of many, many different kinds of evils, and I don't have time to illustrate that, but I could. But certainly earning more money to better your condition is not the same as craving to be rich. To go from one home to another because your family is growing and they need more space, that is different than the craving to be rich. To desire money so you might be able to support the Lord's work is not the same as craving to be rich. But the love of money is a root of many different kinds of evils, and what you need to do is to slay that beast of covetousness that is coiled in the human heart like a snake, wanting to choke you. Notice what the Bible has to say about it.

Why is it such a deceitful thing? Well, as I mentioned, we need money, but here's the thing. When you love money, what you'll discover is money will speak louder to you than God. Furthermore, you will be content not with godliness, that's not what will delight you as Paul explains later—it's not what will turn you on. What will really delight you is a big paycheck. That's where your mind will be. That's where your heart will be. That's where your schemes will be. And so, contentment is the second principle.

The third principle is faith. Notice as we turn the page in our Bibles to 1 Timothy 6:17, it says these words: "As for the rich in this present age," Paul is no longer talking about those who simply desire to be rich. He's talking about those who are rich. By the way, what comes to mind when you read that phrase, "As for the rich in this present age"? I immediately think of people who have more money than I do. Is that what you do, too? Do you think, "Well, I may have hundreds or a few thousand," but we think of those who are millionaires. Oh, that's whom Paul is talking to. Well, my friend, if you are employed and have food on the table, and if you have clothes and you live in a decent place, you're rich. I'm rich in comparison to the kinds of situations that Paul was writing to, so don't wiggle out.

If you are here today and you don't have a job and you are wondering whether or not you can pay your bills, then maybe this phrase doesn't apply to you, but the principle still does, so let's include all of ourselves in this. "As for the rich in this present age, charge them not to be haughty." Why would a rich man be haughty? It's because a rich man says, "I don't need you. I don't need to go to church. I don't need your fellowship because, after all, I am totally independent. I am a self-made man." Right? So he warns them not to be haughty or to set their hopes on the uncertainty of riches. Boy, didn't God ever show us the uncertainty of riches during the stock market crash? God loves to do that because there are always those who say, "Well, it'll always be there." No, maybe it won't be there. "Nor to set their hopes on the uncertainty of riches, but on God, who richly provides us with everything to enjoy." You hope in God.

This is huge. You know the name George Müller? He lived in the 1800s and was a contemporary of D.L. Moody. Müller had about eight or nine orphanages in Bristol, England. You can read about this even on the internet if you don't want to read his biography, even though the biography is great. What he did is, he supplied all this money without mentioning money to anybody. All that he did was pray.

Some people think that's what we should do, but actually I need to tell you there's nothing wrong with outlining needs as we shall do, [though] not today, but we will do that to this congregation to inform you as to where we are and why we need your help. But Müller did that and he said he did it, and he fed them. I mean there are so many stories of where the kids sat down at the table and there was nothing to eat, and there was a knock on the door and somebody was bringing a cart of groceries. It was one miracle after another after another, but he said he did it to prove that God can be trusted to three different groups.

First of all, there were young people who didn't know that they could trust God. Secondly, he said there were business people, and those business people thought they had to cheat in order to live, and what he needed to do was to try to show them that no, you don't, because God is able. And then he said there were old people who feared that, in their old age—and in those days there was no social security, and there were no old folks' homes or retirement centers as there are today, that somehow their needs would not be met—and Müller said that he wanted to demonstrate that God can be trusted.

What does this principle mean to you? If I were to take a poll of those who are going through times of financial hardship, you'd probably tell me, "Pastor, I pray about it all the time." And I'd believe you. I'm going to ask you to take a step beyond that. Instead of praying about it, just simply give it to God. Transfer the burden from your heart and give it to God, and just say, "God, I can't handle this." It's not a matter of prayer anymore because prayer is sometimes so easy to give [prayer] in unbelief, and you're just praying because you do not believe anything. When it comes to transferring it and committing it, that becomes a different story. And why is it that God gives us the uncertainty of riches? It's so that we might stop trusting riches and [instead] hope in God.

I must hurry on. The next principle is generosity. 1 Timothy 6:18–19 says, "They are to do good, to be rich in good works," Now there's a way in which all of us can be rich! "to be generous and ready to share, thus storing up treasure for themselves as a good foundation for the future, so that they may take hold of that which is truly life."

You know, I hope you never get over the Bible. It is an unbelievable book. I just read this and I say, "My, what a book," for a couple of reasons. First of all, notice when it comes to giving, the first reason to give is not so The Moody Church can keep its lights on, so we can pay salaries, so we can fund missionaries. That's not the first reason to give. The Bible nowhere is critical of investments. It is very critical of bad investments, but whether you're talking about Jesus or Paul, they're repeatedly talking about money and good investments.

A good investment is one that, number one, has security. It is absolutely secure. It is not subject to the stock market, and number two, it has a high rate of return. Those are the only investments the Bible approves, and Paul is approving it here. He told them what they must do is to be rich in good works, and then to give and to share, so they might store up treasure for themselves as a good foundation for the future; so that they would take hold of that which is life, indeed, and the future has to do with heaven. That's what Jesus said. He said, "Put your money in heaven where moth and rust does not corrupt, where thieves cannot break through and steal, and you've made a very wise investment." Why? It is totally secure. It has a high rate of interest, and you know what? You are doing this for yourself. Self-interest should definitely be the reason why we give.

I can imagine when we take an offering or we explain the needs of The

Moody Church there are some people who say, "Oh, there they go again. That's all the church wants is money. Money, money, money, money." Listen, if you have that attitude, I have a couple of things to say to you just between you and me. Nobody else needs to listen to this.

Number one, keep your money. That's number one. We don't want it and God doesn't need it. Number two, why don't you repent of the fact that you do not understand you are not giving it to us? You are storing up for yourself a treasure and a foundation. Notice this is what the text says. This is what amazes me about the Bible. Look here, it says that they may store up "treasure for themselves" (1 Timothy 6:19). We are giving you the opportunity of making a wise investment for yourself, so that you might meet your money again in eternity. Again, I marvel at the Bible. Look at this. What does money promise? Oh, if you've got lots of money, then for sure you're going to have life. You can have homes all over the world. That's what money promises. Notice Paul says that if you give, you'll lay up for yourself a treasure of that which is truly life. You'll lay up a treasure of godliness and an investment in heaven that is truly life.

Well, there's another principle, but I'm going to have to give that to you some other time because I want to get to this business of marriages, and time goes by so rapidly—so quickly.

Let me move to the end. Do you remember that passage of Scripture that was read to us today and it says, "What more shall I say?" Do you remember that Eric read that from Hebrews 11? There was a young preacher who began with that and said, "What more shall I say?" and someone in the back row said, "Try 'Amen,'" so I'm always a little concerned when that Scripture is read.

Oh, marriages. Number one, and these are all "L's" so you can remember them. Let's go over them quickly.

Number one, listen to each other. What happens in arguments is nobody listens. Immediately, the other spouse is there to correct, to judge, to improve on what is being said, and that's a disaster. You listen to each other. There's nothing you can do for your spouse to give her or him more respect than to simply hear him out totally, without even thinking of how you're going to respond or how quickly you're going to respond—to just let them speak, speak, speak, and listen not only to the words, but also to their hearts. Gentlemen, listen to your wives. You may not agree with them, but you have to hear them. Wives, listen to your husbands totally, and when one is finished, you don't answer right away. You go for a cup of tea and then you come back and you discuss it rationally. Do you remember the verse of Scripture you should have on your refrigerator from Proverbs 26:20? It says, "Where there is no wood the fire goes out." Another story. Listen.

Now a marriage counselor, who knows a lot more about this than I do and I don't know. I'm just quoting— When somebody has counseled couples for years, I always listen to what they have to say— he says that he has observed that, in conflict, women are generally critical and men are lazy. I don't know. I'm just quoting somebody else here. I have nothing to do with it. I'm just reporting. Listen to each other.

We must hurry along. Number two, in the process of listening, learn. That's number two. Learn. There are so many good books about spending plans. Get with a couple that has wisdom. Talk to our pastor of families who has books on budgets, and learn from the past. Learn from your mistakes. Learn from where you are going, and learn and learn and, learn how important that is. If you don't have employment, I have a full-time job for you right now, and the full-time job is to, full-time, look for employment. I know this is easy for me to say, but don't look only in your field. Be willing to do something else. I admire a man whom I know who is very, very highly qualified, and he is working at Jewel stacking groceries. I admire that, and so does God.

This is a very difficult time economically. Talk to our people. We have a re-employment committee here at The Moody Church, and our desire is to be able to help you in terms of employment. I don't know all the things that we can do, but we will do whatever we can to help you during this very difficult time. But sit down and make a spending plan that the two of you can agree on and come to some kind of agreement regarding finances, so that instead of finances being the thing that drives you apart, let the financial issue be that which brings you together. The Bible says in Proverbs 14:23, "In all toil there is profit, but mere talk tends only to poverty." There are all kinds of Proverbs that speak to this issue of money. Be teachable under this "learn" experience.

Number three, lean. Lean on God. Do you think God abandons you when things get difficult? Do you think God says, "Well, you know, you're in this mess, and I'm just going to leave you there." Well, He may leave you there to teach you some lessons, but if you are a teachable person, God knows that also, and God is there to help us in our need. He's there to help us as a church and as individuals. Our trust is in God and we lean hard on Him. Husbands, it's your responsibility to pray with your wives and to give all these matters to God and to take God's promises and to hang on to them. And if you're looking for another verse to put on your refrigerator, how about 2 Chronicles 16:9? This will bless your soul. The Scripture says the Lord's eyes go to and fro throughout the whole earth, seeking those whose hearts are perfect toward Him that He might greatly fend for them, that He might be strong on behalf of those whose hearts are set on Him. Of course, this is a time of distress. For the world, it's a time of distress, and our eyes need to be set on God.

Finally, I want to say a word to those of us who have employment. What is our responsibility during difficult financial times? Our responsibility is to help. A woman in prayer meeting prayed the other day, and it was so beautiful. She said, "Lord, you spoke not only to Elijah, but you also spoke to the raven to bring him food. And when the Lord needed some money, He not only spoke to Peter, but He spoke to the fish in whose mouth the coin was that they needed." God speaks to those who do not have, and He also speaks to those who have.

I have to tell you that throughout the years, my wife and I have been able to give gifts of money to a lot of different people who have financial needs, and it's wonderful to do it. You don't get a tax credit for it, but the fact that you know about it and God knows about it is so freeing and so liberating to bless others. It really is, and we need to have our eyes and our ears open and see whether or not God is leading into our lives those whom we can bless and those whom we can help. And I know you have done the same and you have experienced the same joy of giving.

Whatever you do, don't die with a lot of money. Give it away before you die. My philosophy is I want to do my givin' while I'm livin' so I'm knowin' where it's goin'. [*laughter*] And whatever you do, don't give your kids a lot. You'll destroy them. If they're needy, give them enough. A woman in prayer meeting just this past Wednesday looked up at me with a big smile and said, "Pastor Lutzer, if I die, half of my money is going to Moody Bible Institute, and half is going to The Moody Church." Well might she smile, by the way. Moody Bible Institute is training missionaries, and The Moody Church is sending missionaries all over the world, helping here in the great city of Chicago, and building families. She is storing up treasure for herself—a good foundation for the future—that she may lay hold of that which is truly life.

Let me ask you something. You claim to be a Christian. Are you generous? Very quickly, visualize a man who has a huge estate. He has absolutely everything, and in this estate he has a servant who is evil. The servant steals from him. The servant is critical of him. The servant hurts others. He is an evil servant. But the man also has a son whom he greatly loves. He is wildly in love with his son, and he says to his son, "Son, I have chosen to love that evil servant with the very same love with which I love you, but in order for me to forgive that servant so that we can have fellowship together, you are going to have to die, and you are going to have to bear the sin and the evil of that servant." That's the gospel, and the Bible says that God loves us even as He loves Christ. I'm not making it up. It's there in John 17:23: "Thou...hast loved them, as thou hast loved me," (KJV) and God says, "That's how much I love you, and that's what I paid to redeem you."

Can you accept a redemption like that, a forgiveness like that, and then be stingy? I don't think so. God says that what He wants to do is to have us lay it all before Him, and to work things out in such a way that, in this business of money, there might be harmony and peace in our homes—whether we have much or little—for His glory. And by the way, some of you who are listening, you maybe never trusted Christ as Savior. You've never trusted that Son. The Bible says, "He that spared not his own Son, but delivered him up for us all, how shall he not with him also freely give us all things?" (Romans 8:32, KJV). I recommend Jesus to you today. He's the one who can reconcile you to God, forgive your sin, make you a child of the King, and then you are also in the mainstream of His eternal blessing.

Let's pray together.

Father, take these thoughts, however scattered, we pray, and use them according to your good will and purpose, and we ask, O Lord Jesus, that you will grant to us the sure knowledge that whether we have little or much in this life, we have an equal opportunity to be faithful and to love you and to serve you. Grant that, O God, we ask in Jesus' name, Amen.

ERWIN W. LUTZER

SERMON SEVEN
THE PUZZLE OF ADDICTIONS

Today's topic is the topic of addictions. Addictions are tearing our families apart. Let me list just a few. First of all, at the top of the list, I put alcoholism. Think of the destruction that has happened because of alcoholism—the family beatings, the family secrets, and the family poverty. I was in Coors Stadium a couple of years ago. Somebody took us to a baseball game there. It was in Denver, I believe. [It was] a gorgeous stadium. In fact, we ate and we could watch the game as we ate, and it dawned on me later that this whole thing was built basically on the backs of alcoholics. Oh, I know there are some people who drink and are not alcoholics, but it's the alcoholics who are selling their homes and pushing their families into poverty to get that drink.

I list also gambling. "Oh," you say, "it's not an addiction." Oh, yes, it is. We don't have time for the stories. I must hurry on.

Drugs. A cocaine addict in New York chained himself to a radiator. He said to himself, "I can't get another fix," and yet he was able somehow to get that radiator loose with his free hand, and eventually took the thing and carried it out on the street for more drugs, and then he said, "Cocaine has a voice. When it calls me, I must go." Think about that.

And I suppose the one we are most conscious of is sexual addictions of various kinds, compulsions too many to list, but I do want to speak about pornography and the internet, just in passing. I told you many years ago that when we got onto the internet in our home (AOL—I always remember it— America Online), the day we hooked up, that night, God gave me a demonic dream. It was horrible. I've only had three in my lifetime, and one was that evening. It was a dream in black and white that I can still describe today.

Three evil spirits had me up against a corner in the house and I was totally paralyzed, and they were destroying me. Can you imagine how I felt when I woke up? I was thankful to God it was only a dream. I interpreted it as a gift from God. What God was saying was, "You now have something in your home that demons can use to destroy you," and whenever I've been tempted to go to the other side of the [internet] and type in some of those other words where sexual material would come up, I think of that dream and that warning from God, and I thank God for that warning.

If you're a parent today and you have children in your home and you don't have filters on your computer because you trust them [your children], could I ask you a question? Tell me later: Which planet do you live on? Which one? Or are you just orbiting somewhere close to Pluto? What do you mean, you trust your children? I've met children who were trusted by their parents who were hooked on pornography. Its power is great and when young people discover it, as they do now at about the age of eleven and twelve, it is a horrendous burden that continues to dog them unless they are intercepted. So, what you need to do is, before you eat—You don't need to eat. You can survive without eating—go to the Moody Church Media website and there we have a link that will help you to identify various software programs that can help your computer have a filter. It's more important that you do that than eating. (Link for Internet Safety: https://moodymedia.org/internet).

But I do need to give you a parenthesis. If you find your children into pornography, don't shame them. There isn't a child in the world who said, "You know, my parents found out and they shamed me, and therefore my appetite for pornography no longer exists." Are you kidding me? Shame becomes the fuel of this addiction, even though it will become more secret, of course, to avoid the shame. What you do is you talk to them, and you confess your own struggles with purity. Haven't we all had them? So, in humility you say, "Look, I want to help you through this because this is a quagmire. This is dangerous stuff that's going to dog you for the rest of your life, so let's work together as a family. Let's talk about these things." Open communication is one of the best ways to prevent addictions, and it's one of the best ways to come out of it. Parents, please don't be so judgmental. Don't you have enough of your own sins to make you humble and broken? I hope you do.

What is an addiction? An addiction is a false promise. It promises you this sense of exhilaration you can have whatever you want. I love the definition that can't be improved upon. No way. This is it: An addiction is nothing more than the self-absorption of sin. It's the self-absorption of sin—the blinding. That's the word I forgot to mention. It's the blinding self-absorption of sin. That's what an addiction is, and what a prison it is. Addictions come along as our friend. [They say,] "Oh, I'll be there, and whenever you need some exhilaration, I'll be there for you, and you can manipulate me, and this god—this idol—is under your control, and you can have it whenever you plan to have it." It comes as a friend, but it ends up being a tremendous tyrant, and it will control you. Jesus was so right when He said if you commit sin, you become its servant, and now you are taking orders from the voices that call you, and you can't get out.

What I'm going to do in the next twenty minutes, with God's help, is wander into Satan's territory and see if we can't win some victories today. Are you in favor of that? Is there anybody who says, "Pastor Lutzer, let's see if Jesus can win some victories today"? [*applause*]

But, of course, we can't do it. I've never felt more helpless than I feel today preaching this message. Who in the world is going to be able to go and untie the knots and deal with the shame and the forgiveness and the deliverance? I can't do it. My sermons can't do it. Wives, you can't do it for your husbands. You probably can't even do it for yourself. God has to come.

Father, I ask in Jesus' name, that you'll make every person listening to this sermon open. We pray that their [ears] and their hearts would be attuned. I pray that no one will leave because of conviction, and [I] ask, Lord Jesus, that by your Spirit, you will do what we wouldn't even think of doing, and that is to come to deliver your people from their sins. That's your work. We trust the Holy Spirit because if the Holy Spirit doesn't do it, we're helpless. Help every man here to pray. Help every woman here to pray. Help every young person and every adult to call on you and say, "God, help us." In Jesus' name, Amen.

The Bible says in the book of Proverbs—and it is so accurate, isn't it?—in chapter 5, verse 22 that, "The iniquities of the wicked ensnare him, and he is held fast in the cords of his sin" (Proverbs 5:22). Don't you like the imagery? That's exactly true: he is bound [held fast] by the cords of his sin. And what are some of those cords? Let me list them for you very quickly.

First of all, there's the cord of euphoria. You see, what the addict does is he goes into this other world that he can stimulate and he can generate; he can leave the world of boredom behind and he can go into this exciting world.

Just the idea of planning his next fix gives him an increase in heart rate as the sensation begins to pulse through his body. Just the thought of it. And the thing is, he can go from this false world to the real world, and nobody even knows it; so nobody knows what he's doing on the weekends. He is able to function, he's able to hold a job, he's able to converse, but in the back [of his mind], all of those other things are going on and he can have it whenever he wants it or plans for it—this sensation, this euphoria.

The second chain that holds him bound is self-worship. Self-worship is known as narcissism. Remember narcissists are very interesting people. They have concern only for themselves. They have no concern for anybody else. Does the alcoholic father who comes home and beats his kids really have sympathy for those children? No, of course he doesn't or he'd stop doing it. What he thinks is, "They have it coming." He can't enter into his wife's pain. He can't enter into the burdens other people bear. He is filled with self—self-worship—and this self-worship causes him tremendous problems, and he's totally unaware of the damage he's doing.

The third is denial. I've told you before that denial isn't just a river in Egypt. Denial exists in all families, but there's nowhere where it's found as much as in an alcoholic family—a drug-infested family, a family where there's immorality or incest going on. The denial is this: First of all, the person who's doing it shifts responsibility. He says, "It's not my fault. It's somebody else's fault. It's my employer's fault. It's my wife's fault. It's circumstances. It's God's fault." So, he fails to take responsibility. He doesn't own what he's doing because he's blind to it. Remember? It's the blinding self-absorption of sin. What a description. So, you see, he lives in this cocoon and the cocoon isolates him and insulates him from all of the lies he has so willingly believed. He loves these lies. He tells himself lies, and he keeps believing these lies.

In the New Testament, there is the light/darkness motif. Jesus used it. Someday, I want to study this even in more detail. Jesus said, "Men love darkness rather than light because their deeds are evil." He said that. "Men love darkness because," He said, "they don't want to come to the light lest their deeds be exposed."

Come with me to Mexico more than forty years ago. I had a sister and brother-in-law, who were missionaries there, and so I went to visit them. We stayed in a motel, and this motel had a kitchenette in it, [and had] two or three bedrooms. We went out one evening and when we came back and flipped on the light—there must have been a hundred roaches with all of their aunts and uncles and kids on that kitchen counter—and they just scattered like that. In two seconds, you couldn't see a roach. They knew exactly where the cracks were. They knew where the holes were. And everybody was running for cover.

Maybe some of you are feeling like that today. You may be listening on the internet or you may be listening by radio and you say, "This is going to get very difficult for me," and you'd like to bail out. There's a big difference though between you and a roach. Let me tell you that you, my friend, are created in God's image. You are important. You're going to live somewhere forever. You are a human being in the image of God, and you are loved by God. Would you let God put His arms around you today and pull you close and say, "Come to me. Don't let your addiction draw you away from me, but may it be the means by which you are brought to me."

With that background of light and darkness, let's go into the characteristics of darkness. We're in 1 John. I could have used many different passages to preach this because the whole storyline of the Bible has to do with sin and redemption. Once we understand [that] an addiction is the self-absorption of sin, then there is hope. If it's just a sickness, we have no guarantee God always heals sicknesses, but sin—that's another matter. He's got a good cure for that. But notice it says in 1 John 1:5–7, "This is the message we have heard from him and proclaim to you, that God is light, and in him is no darkness at all. If we say we have fellowship with him while we walk in darkness, we lie and do not practice the truth. But if we walk in the light, as he is in the light, we have fellowship with one another."

Folks, I can't go any farther than that without making a comment. Are your Bibles open? Do you see the text? Do you remember some grammar? (A kid said to another kid who made a grammatical error, "Where's your grammar?" He said, "She's up there with grandpa.") Do you remember the meaning of the word antecedent? When you have a pronoun, doesn't it refer to the antecedent? Now listen. Let's read this again. 1 John 1:7 says, "If we walk in the light, as God is in the light," that's the "he" very clearly, you'll notice it says, "we have fellowship with one another." Most interpreters say, "Oh, that means I have fellowship with you, and you have fellowship with me," but that's not the antecedent. The antecedent is God. "If we walk in the light," and *light* here refers to God's purity and His holiness, "as God is in the light," guess what? "We have fellowship one with another." We have fellowship with

God and God has fellowship with us. Can it get any better than that?

If you were to die, what would you like to have on your tombstone? I think the greatest honor you can imagine is a tombstone that says, "He (or she) walked with God." I think that would be the greatest honor, and it won't be on mine because I don't think I am worthy of it, but can you imagine it?

Last evening, I was outside praying. There were the stars and I thought, "Wow. To walk with God." If I accomplish nothing—if I don't preach any sermons, if I don't' write any books—but if I can just walk with God and He has fellowship with me and I with Him, that's the end of it. I mean, there's nothing more.

Notice though: What are the characteristics of darkness? I'm going to give you some characteristics of darkness that are in verse six and then we're going to go into the characteristics of light. Then I'm going to paint the picture of how you go from darkness to light. Aren't you glad you joined us today?

First of all, what are the characteristics of walking in darkness? Shame. Some of you were brought up in what could be called a shame-based home where there is alcoholism and drugs and you had to keep the secret for the rest of the family. You have lived with shame, and that shame dogs you—that is all false shame, by the way. It's shame imposed upon you. Parents have so much power to impose false shame on children. I could give examples, but there are some things you and I have done that we should be ashamed about. Some shame is good. It should lead us to God, but imagine living your whole life in shame.

Secondly, fear of being discovered and fear of giving up your addiction. I have talked to people who have said, "I am my addiction. The thought of me doing without this bottle is unthinkable. It is there when I'm rich and when I'm poor—and usually it makes me poor when I'm rich. But it is there for me." This addiction becomes, you see, the basis of our identity. Some of you are into sexuality in various forms. You say, "The sexuality is who I am. How do you expect me to give that up?" You fear what would happen if God were to invade your life.

Let me give you a third characteristic of darkness, and [one] that is huge. It is self-deception. In fact, the Bible says here that if we say we have no sin, we make Him a liar. That's in 1 John 1:10. Elsewhere it says we deceive ourselves. In fact, 1 John 1:6 says, "If we say we have fellowship with him while we walk in darkness, we lie." Self-deception is huge.

How does an addict live with self-deception? I have a couple of suggestions of self-deception that he lives with. First of all, "I can quit whenever I want. I'm in charge." That's a lie. Of course, you're not in charge. The addiction is in charge. You're like Mark Twain who said, "Of course, I can give up smoking. I've done it a thousand times." There's the self-deception that you are in charge when you're not.

Let me give you another, and that is consequences. You may say, "I can handle the consequences. I'll follow the devil today and I'll deal with God tomorrow and handle the consequences then." Somebody has said that a man who is committing adultery, who is being unfaithful to his wife, is like somebody who chooses to jump out of the sixtieth floor of a high-rise. After he gets up enough nerve and jumps out of the sixtieth floor, he says to himself as he passes the twenty-fifth floor, "Oh, this is great. The exhilaration really is wonderful," but he's by the twenty-fifth floor and you know where he's going—onto the street.

You see, addicts rationalize it all. They say, "I can take care of it." So, what you have is shame, fear, and huge, massive self-deception.

Well, if that's what walking in darkness is, what does walking in light mean? You'll notice it says, "God is light and in him is no darkness at all. If we say we have fellowship with him while we walk in darkness," and if we deny that part of us that is dark, we can't have fellowship with Him, "we lie and we do not practice the truth. But if we walk in the light, as he is in the light..." What does that mean? What does it mean to walk in the light?

First of all, light reveals to us who we are. We used to, as children, when we'd go to town— Do you realize I was born on a farm six miles from a town of seventy-five people? Going to town was great. The town had a store where we could buy some candy and gum, but it also had a streetlight and as kids, we could move away from the streetlight and there would be this long shadow. In fact, we couldn't even see the end of the shadow, but as we came closer to the streetlight the shadow became shorter and shorter, and then when we stood right under the streetlight, basically there was no shadow— You see, light reveals who we are. Because it's not who I say I am; it's who God says I am. Light comes, you see, and darkness is what I think of myself, and light is what God thinks of me. He sees me in the light. So as I come to the light with my darkness, the shadows become shorter, and suddenly I'm revealed as to who I am. And as I stand there, I finally acknowledge that God is right about me. But if I deny the shadows, and if I don't admit there are shadows, then I can't walk in the light.

You know, light is fascinating. I'm just amazed at the light of the sun. I have a number of different suits, all of which are blue, and several of which have stripes. I don't know how that happened, but that's just the way it is. Sometimes when I dress, I take a pair of pants and a suit coat and I sit there and I look at them and I think, "Yeah, they are a match." But when I go into the sunlight I say, "Oy-yoy-yoy! This isn't a match." [*laughter*] It's amazing what light does.

In the very same way, God's light shines upon us and suddenly, we begin to see what we're doing. Suddenly, we see the consequences. Suddenly, we see what we're doing to other people. But mind you, we'll never see it unless we come to the light. The rationalizations are too deep and too strong. It [light] reveals who we are and it reveals our path. "Thy word is a lamp unto my feet, and a light unto my path" (Psalm 119:105, KJV). You're walking along in life and you don't know where to step next when you're in darkness.

By the way, I hope you learn to love the Bible. Are there any Bible lovers out there? [*applause*] I mean, you take for example a Proverb and there's also a verse in Psalms— and don't ask me for the references because I don't know them right now, but I promise you they are there, and I'm paraphrasing now. It says, "The wicked stumble but they don't know what they are stumbling over" (Proverbs 4:19). Of course not, because they are walking in darkness.

You know, when you stumble on something in the darkness, you don't know whether you stumbled on a stone, a piece of concrete, or a piece of gold. You don't know, and here are people who think that as long as you have lots of money, and lots of sex, and lots of drink, you are supposed to be happy. When they're not happy then they say, "Well, I need some drugs, too, to cover the emptiness that my life creates." But this has to be the path, so they keep stumbling, stumbling, stumbling, and they have no idea why they are stumbling or what they are stumbling after. Light reveals our path.

Now listen. Some of you say, "Pastor Lutzer, if I were to take this sermon really seriously, like God wants me to take it, I'd have to break a sinful relationship I'm involved in," because you're living in an unholy bed. And you say to yourself, like one woman said, "It's unthinkable for me to give up what I am doing. Ask me to pick up a building and move it to the other side of the street." Listen, when you come to the light, God begins to show you the path—and it is a path—and the light will help you, and the light not only ends up revealing our path, but it also ends up also showing our destination.

The Bible says, in the book of Revelation, that someday, when we are with God, we're going to dwell with Him in light. It says regarding the New Jerusalem, that there is no need of the sun or of the moon to shine upon it for the Lord God Almighty is the temple of it, and the Lamb is the light thereof, and it says those who believe in Christ will walk with Him in light.

Live in darkness? Don't receive Jesus Christ as Savior—eternal darkness. Receive Jesus as Savior—eternal light. Could the contrast be any greater?

So, how do we make the transition? If we walk in the light, it reveals who we are. It reveals our path. It reveals our destination. How do we make the transition? [Here is] some practical, pastoral help here.

Number one, we must come to the light when we feel the heat. You see, there are some of you here today who are going to continue to hide, and the reason that you are going to continue to hide is because you still think that your secret—well-guarded that it is—is yours to manage, and if revealed, will hurt you.

On Saturday morning, I was listening to a program on WMBI and they spoke with a man who has helped more than three thousand couples overcome adultery and pornography. One of the things he said that I often suspected, but I never heard anyone say, is this: He said most people who are delivered are those who were caught. We usually don't come on our own.

I remember a friend of mine who was involved in an adulterous relationship. He is a very close friend—among my top five or six friends in the world—and he told me later, "A year or two ago, I wanted to come to you, but I couldn't." Oh, he would have spared himself so much grief. Of course, he was involved in this, and there were consequences, but what happened after was far worse. Don't wait until you're caught. Come to the light. It's better to do it that way because it's only going to get worse.

This past week, I received a letter from a woman who said that her brother almost died of a drug overdose seven years ago, but she said it so woke him up that today, not only has he been sober for seven years, but he's leading people to faith in Jesus Christ. Why does it take almost death before you come to the light? I hope this message enables you to feel the heat so you don't have to end up splattered against the pavement before you wake up.

First of all, what we must do is we must come when we feel the heat. Parenthetically, I should have mentioned it earlier, if you are living with an addict, you really ought to go to one of the various groups that will provide help for you. I received a letter from someone who said that Al-Anon, for example, saved her life. There are groups that help you to understand the chaos you are dealing with. So, anyway, we must come when we feel the heat.

Secondly, we must come and agree with God. You say, "Well, Pastor Lutzer, get specific." Well, I think I was pretty specific, but now I'm going to get even more specific.

First John 1:8 says, "If we say we have no sin, we deceive ourselves." You see, what John is saying is there are those who walk in the light. They are up to date with God and they believe they are in fellowship with God. God has fellowship with them, and they begin to think, "You know, I'm perfect." In fact, there are whole denominations that teach that you can be perfect. Could you imagine, ladies, living with a man who believed he was perfect? It's not a pretty picture. I remember meeting a man like that. His wife wasn't at all convinced of his perfection.

It says, "If we say that we have no sin (We say, "Oh, I'm so holy because I walk in the light, I have no sin now."), we deceive ourselves" because even those who walk in the light still have some darkness that's still there, too. Human beings are very interesting.

But now notice it says in 1 John 1:9, "If we confess our sins, he is faithful and just to forgive us our sins and to cleanse us from all (each individual) unrighteousness." This was written to Christians, but it's going to apply to those of you who are investigating Christianity, to those of you who are on the fringes. I'm going to apply it to you in just a moment, but first of all, to those of you who are Christians, this is what it means to confess: It means you agree with God. You agree with God and you say, "What I'm doing is sin; it's displeasing to you, Lord; it is creating darkness between you and me, and this darkness causes me to run." You know, there are people who do not want to come to church, and the reason they don't is because this light begins to shine on them and they don't want to come to the light and it's very, very uncomfortable.

When you confess your sins, you agree that this is sin; you agree that God has a right to take it from your life forever; you agree totally and say, "Whatever, Lord, you ask me to do, I'm going to do it because I am going to fully and totally agree with you on everything." That's the way you walk in the light. Those of you who are believers will know—and it's true of my experience also—that every day we have to come and we have to say, "Lord, today I want to walk in the light." And when we walk in darkness, as we sometimes do, we have to bring that darkness to the Lord and say, "Lord, here I am, and I am going to claim this verse that you are going to forgive me and cleanse me."

Don't just stop at forgiveness. You ladies who have had an abortion, if you stop at forgiveness you're going to be haunted even though you are forgiven, because the text says He is faithful and just to forgive. You need to also accept the cleansing. The cleansing means our consciences become clear in God's presence, and so we not only are forgiven, but we sense that we are forgiven and we stand in that forgiveness, because the text says if we agree with God, this is known as repentance.

The man who helped three thousand couples get out of adultery and pornography said that, at the end of the day, what is really necessary is deep repentance. I thought, "Amen, that's what's necessary." All of us need to deeply repent, and we need to repent every day, and we have to confess that we agree with God if we're going to walk in the light.

Now, for those of you who have never trusted Christ as Savior, I need to clarify something. You don't necessarily begin by confessing your sins because there's no way you could remember all of your sins. Any one of us could not possibly remember all of our sins. Could you imagine me sitting down and saying, "I want to remember all of my sins"? I mean, I'd have to sit there for at least a year and a half and write them on ten notepapers and then I still wouldn't have a clue whether I had remembered and listed all of my sins.

So, what you need to do is to transfer your trust to Jesus. Now, I've got some good news for you. Boy, are you in the right place today if you are investigating Christianity, because this is what the Bible says. It says when Jesus died on the cross, His death was a sacrifice for sinners, and catch this, when we believe in Him as our substitute, having died in our place, and we receive Him as our Savior, personally—the Bible says we are translated from the domain of darkness into the domain of His dear Son (Colossians 1:13).

You see, before you can begin to even walk in the light, you have to be translated into the domain of light—the domain of His dear Son. And God alone can translate you from the kingdom of darkness, where demons rule and where all the rationalizations take place, to remove you from that kingdom and put you into the kingdom of His beloved Son where you will still have battles as a Christian. There's no question about it. We'll have battles. We'll wrestle with lust and greed and some of these sins until we die, but you are on the winning side, and you know enough about the Christian life to know how to walk in light, to walk in fellowship, to confess your sins when God brings it to your attention, and to be free.

There is something else walking in the light means. It is not only coming to the light when we feel the heat—confessing our sins—but also it means we connect with other people. Notice what the text says back in 1 John 1:3. It says, "That which we have seen and heard we proclaim also to you, so that you too may have fellowship with us." In this context, he's talking about fellowship with other believers.

One day, there was a man in Colorado giving a seminar to help people overcome pornography. I wish I could have attended it, but I was giving a seminar simultaneously on a different topic, so I had lunch with him and said, "Tell me what you told them." I was expecting some brand-new, great truth that was going to be revolutionary. What he said was, "The best way to overcome is through healthy honest relationships." You can't get out of it alone. You need others. You see, that's why we have the men's fraternity at The Moody Church, and that's why we have TMC Communities. It's not as if we do these things because we want to keep people off the streets and find something they can do. We want you to be able to connect with other believers, and what you must do is take advantage of these opportunities. Because guess what? You can get in that pit alone, but you need others to help you get out of that pit—because you can't do it alone.

Therefore, what we encourage you to do greatly is to make sure you end up in those relationships that are going to be healthy. It is a journey out of addictions. The journey begins by receiving Christ as Savior. It begins by agreeing with God. It begins by confessing to people whom you have wronged. It begins by having your eyes open to the consequences and to giving up this crazy illusion that you are in charge when you're not. What it means, therefore, is that through humility and repentance before God and, as necessary, before others, you finally come out of the darkness.

I've never yet met a person who was in an addiction where God delivered him or her, and they said, "You know, I'm delivered from my addiction, but it wasn't worth the cost. The exposure was just too much," or "It just hurt too much." No, no, no. Imagine being free. Imagine walking in the light.

So this God—about whom we know only so little, yet He has revealed Himself in His Holy Word—we have fellowship with Him, and He has fellowship with us because He loves us and He wants to connect with us even more than we want to connect with Him. Could it get any better than that? Could it? I don't think so.

Finally, what you need to do is to get found. I love the little book Robert Fulghum wrote entitled, *All I Really Needed to Know I Learned in Kindergarten*. He said that in [one] October when he was a child, he and his friends would play hide and seek under the leaves. He said, "There was always one kid who hid so well that nobody could find him. Eventually, the others gave up on him. When he finally showed up, they would explain there is a hiding but there is also a finding, and he was not to hide in such a way that he could not be found."

Then Fulghum says, "As I write this, the neighborhood game goes on and there is a kid under a pile of leaves in the yard just under my window. He's been there a long time now and everybody else is found and they are about to give up on him. I considered going out to the pile of leaves and telling them where he was hiding, and I thought even about setting the leaves on fire to drive him out. [*laughter*] Finally, I just yelled, 'Get out, kid. Get found.' And it scared him so bad he probably started crying and ran home to tell his mother. Sometimes it's hard to know how to be helpful."

Today, God led you here. Today, God led you to listen to this message by whatever means you're listening to it. Get found. Open up to God. Tell Him you want to walk in the light.

Father, take these words, we ask, and burn them into the souls of all those for whom they were intended, and let us not go until we walk in the light.

Before I conclude this message and this prayer, I'm talking now to you who have heard it. Would you talk to God right now? If you've never received Christ as Savior, open your life to Him and say, "Lord Jesus, today I receive you as Savior." Would you do that? "I believe you died for me. I want to be translated from the kingdom of darkness to the kingdom of light." Tell God that right now. You want to be free. For those of you who are believers and you're walking in darkness, come to the light right now. Tell God that.

Father, we need you. Amen.

SERMON 8

THE PUZZLE OF ABUSE

The topic today is abuse. And I need to tell you abuse occurs in all kinds of families—good families, supposedly good, as well the ones where we might expect it. As a pastor, the letters I receive that are most heartbreaking—sometimes I am almost unable to read them—are stories of abuse that people write to me, sometimes asking for counsel or simply wanting prayer. They come from women in destructive relationships, children growing up in homes where there is division and strife and all kinds of abuse, and it's everywhere. Yes, there is physical abuse: slapping, hitting, kicking, whipping, shoving, pushing, punching—intended to humiliate and intended to control.

Then there's also verbal abuse, which can be even more destructive: swearing, name-calling, obscenities, belittling, downgrading, and shaming. It's all there. And then I think of that terrible thing called sexual abuse. What we need to do is to realize that when a child is sexually abused, he or she will believe that their only value to adults and to others is their sexuality. So, as a result of that experience, they will tend to mimic again the type of abuse they received as a child, even as they go into adulthood.

Just recently, I received an email from someone who told me the story of a woman whom I came to know many, many years ago who was visiting this church. She had two children. Her husband died and she remarried. Now she has a twenty-year-old daughter who had a child out of wedlock. The daughter confesses what the mother suspected, namely, that her stepfather had sexually abused her for nine years. Just think of this situation the mother is in. Her husband, now, is in jail, thankfully, where he should be; but on the other hand, she is the breadwinner in the home. She's about to lose her house and she is spending her time in a job, trying to earn a little bit of money at Home Depot stacking shelves. I read that and I thought, "What a broken world in which we live." The stories, of course, are endless of men seducing young boys to go into homosexuality. We could go on in terms of what all that means but we must hurry.

The devil, of course, plays a tremendous part in all of this. Because, you see, you and I are born with a desire to be valued, and if we are not valued, we will find that value. A sexually abused child will find that value in destructive sexual relationships. We all want to mean something to somebody, and abuse goes right to the heart of who we are. And the devil likes it because he wants us to think we are junk, that God doesn't love us, that we're damaged goods, and we have no future. That's the lie of the devil.

What are some of the characteristics of those who are abused? Well, of course, there is oftentimes rage and anger. And because this rage and anger is unacknowledged, what you have is, of course, all of it lying there that is going to come out at some point in a future relationship.

You also have numbness of emotions. After all, you had to turn your emotions off. You couldn't deal with the pain, and because you couldn't deal with it, you had to simply shut down emotionally and check out. That's why abuse carries on from generation to generation. Here's an angry man (or it could be an angry woman) and when he abuses his children, he has no feelings for them. He does not enter into the pain that he's doing. It's all fully justified in his own mind.

So, you have those characteristics, and then in addition to that, you have a great deal of guilt because, remember, the abuser always blames you. It's your fault for what is happening. And then if that isn't enough, you also have a tremendous amount of shame. And so, you hide in the shadows. You hide from your friends. You hide from yourself. You even hope you can hide from God.

What about the characteristics of the abuser? One of the great and first characteristics I have listed is, number one, that he doesn't think he is an abuser. Maybe he was brought up in an abusive [home] and he thinks that's the way it should be, or likely, he simply justifies what he's doing. He lives in denial and you can't reason with him or her, at least [not] very well.

Another characteristic is that he is very narcissistic. Because of that narcissism, he blames others. "You made me hit you," he says. "It's your fault

I'm swearing at you. It's your fault I broke your wrist." It's always your fault. Because of his narcissism, he takes no responsibility for what he's doing. And of course, oftentimes, he's charming. You have to understand abusers sometimes are charmers. It's a difficult story to tell, but frequently when abuse happens and someone points out that a person is abusive, people say, "I don't believe he was abusive. Look at how nice he is." Yes, remember, it is not important for him to be good, but it is very important for him to appear good—so, he can be charming and helpful. He's the kind of man all of the other women in the church wish they had married.

There's another characteristic, and that is he is filled with self-righteousness because, you see, he's the only one who has a standard. He says, "You know the reason I slapped that kid is that, in my home, it's not going to be this way," and, "You deserve to be punished because you overspent." So, he'll holler or he'll hit, and on and on it goes.

[Here's] a word to those of you who are listening as abusers. Whether it's here in the sanctuary, whether it's by the internet, whether it's on the radio, or you are hearing this message on CD, I have a word for you. Would you get help real soon? I mean, like by tomorrow, because it's never going to get better. Don't you dare believe that lie that you're going to change, because you won't. You've told yourself the lie before, and you don't have the power to [change]. And if you have been abused, please do the same thing—get help.

I received a letter from a woman who said, "You know, I'm in an abusive relationship. I had to leave. I went to a women's shelter where all of the abused women are, and I discovered there they were abusing their own children." Break the cycle in the name of Jesus.

Well, we have some work to do today and so what I'm going to ask you to do is to pray. Pray that God will speak to us. Pray that all of the defenses and the rationale that an abuser or someone who is abused might have might be broken down in the presence of Jesus who loves us and died for us. Would you join me as we pray?

Father, I ask in Jesus' name that Satan, who loves abuse because he's a lover of evil—may his power be broken. May those who are bound in shame and in hurt come out of the shadows into the light of your Word, into the light of your presence, and may there be transformation. Lord, speak, and may each person right now pray that you will speak to him or to her and to me. We pray in Jesus' name, Amen.

I know it takes a great deal of effort and time to overcome the effects of abuse. I know that. That's why we have this hotline ministry called "Set Free," but on the other hand, I want to jumpstart the process. I want to help you on your journey today, and to do that, would you take your Bibles please, and turn to Isaiah 52? We're going to very quickly walk through what Jesus did for us, and then we're going to apply it to the situation of abuse and we'll see its relevance. Normally, we think of Isaiah 53, but I'm beginning at chapter 52 and then we'll get into chapter 53.

Chapter 52 is speaking about Jesus in verse 13. It says, "Behold, my servant shall act wisely; he shall be high and lifted up, and shall be exalted. As many were astonished at you," and now it describes why they were, "his appearance was so marred, beyond human semblance, and his form beyond that of the children of mankind" (Isaiah 52:13–14). Let's stop there.

First, number one, the abuse that Jesus received. Imagine it. His form was so marred, He didn't look human. It says [it] in two different ways in the text we read. When the soldiers were beating Jesus, and people walked by, the question wasn't, "Is He the Son of God?" The question was, "Is that a human being?" That was the question. As a matter of fact, Jesus was so beaten—and Mel Gibson's movie helps us here—that people probably walked by and said, "What is that thing that you are hitting?" Jesus experienced abuse. The Bible says that He shall sprinkle many nations. That's probably a reference to His position as a priest to giving healing and forgiveness. The sprinkling of water was symbolic of forgiveness. You can also translate it, "He shall startle many nations." Either translation works, because people are going to be surprised because the mouths of kings, the Bible says, are going to be closed. The whole issue is [that] they're going to look back and say, "Oh, you mean that man who was so ordinary was the Messiah? Oh, we can't believe it." They had no idea whom they were beating.

Abuser, I have a word for you. You have no idea who the child is that you are abusing. You have no idea who that little girl is that you are sexually molesting. You have no idea. Created in the image of God, special to God. Oh, I know Jesus was in an entirely different category, but the principle applies. Jesus was abused and the people who did the abusing, at one level, didn't know whom they were hitting.

Let's go on now and let's look at the rejection of Jesus. This is in Isaiah 53. If you are underlining your Bible, as you should from time to time, notice the

Bible says in Isaiah 53:3, "He was despised and rejected by men." Why was Jesus rejected? It was for a couple of reasons [that are] right in the text. First of all, it was because of His background, for He grew up from a young plant and a root out of dry ground. Jesus came from Nazareth. That was like being born in the projects of Chicago. It was the place of which people asked, "Can any good thing come out of Nazareth?" The genealogy of Jesus was suspect and, you see, because of that, He was a root out of dry ground. You wouldn't expect Messiah to be born in a genealogy that contains the harlot Rahab, and then you have, of course, also Uriah's wife, Bathsheba, and David, and you wouldn't expect that. A root out of dry ground—who is He? Can any good thing come out of Nazareth? So, He was rejected because of His background.

He was rejected also because of His appearance. You'll notice it says in the middle of verse 2 that He had no form or majesty that we should look at Him. He didn't come looking like a king, and then it says, "And there was no beauty that we should desire him." I love Jesus, but I want to tell you frankly there's no evidence in Scripture that Jesus was handsome or that He was striking in His appearance. He was very, very ordinary. There was no beauty that we should desire Him. I mean, if you talked to Him, I'm sure His beauty came out and you realized you weren't talking just to a human being, but in the run of things, He was not the most handsome person, He wasn't the one you would choose. There was no beauty that we should desire Him.

He was also rejected because He was a man of sorrows. You'll notice in Isaiah 53:3 it says He was a "man of sorrows." After all, who wants to be around a man of sorrows? We want to be around people who are happy, happy, happy, happy, but He's "a man of sorrows and acquainted with grief." And that's why we sing:

> "Man of sorrows! what a name;
> For the Son of God who came;
> Ruined sinners to reclaim!
> Hallelujah, what a Savior!"

And so, for these reasons, Jesus was rejected. He was abused and He was rejected, but now I want us to look at the burden that He carried. For this we'll go to Isaiah 53:4, "Surely he has borne our griefs and carried our sorrows; yet we esteemed him stricken, smitten by God, and afflicted. But he was pierced for our transgressions; he was crushed for our iniquities." Wait a moment.

What's happening here? Look at Jesus there in the garden. Look at His sorrows. Look at His grief. Is that His grief? No, that's my grief. That's your grief. He's dying for us in our place. You'll notice it says, "He was pierced for our transgressions; he was crushed for our iniquities." What about that iniquity? What about those transgressions? Those weren't His transgressions. Those were my transgressions. Those are your transgressions. He was dying for sinners. He was dying for us. That's what Jesus was doing. That's why when Rembrandt painted his wonderful picture, *The Raising of the Cross*, he painted himself as one of the people crucifying Jesus, and that was theologically right. We are in this text. I was there when they crucified my Lord. I was there. I'm there in the text. My transgressions. My sorrows. He bore all that.

No wonder we have dysfunctional families. Look at what it says in Isaiah 53:6: "All we like sheep have gone astray; we have turned—every one—to his own way; and the LORD has laid on him the iniquity of us all." You know, sheep will be going along and they'll be following the shepherd, and one sheep is following the other, and one ornery sheep gets off the track and goes in this direction, and all the other ones follow. And that's the way it was in some of your homes. The father got off the track [and] into drink and immorality, and the whole family began to take that direction. We've all scattered, but the Good Shepherd is there.

By the way, always be impressed with the accuracy of Scripture. You'll notice it says here [that] the Lord has laid on Him [Jesus] the iniquity of us all. There was no iniquity in Jesus. You'll never find that in the Bible, but iniquity was laid on Him. God reckoned my iniquity and my sin and my shame, and He laid it on Jesus so that His grief and His sorrow and His shame were all mine. And if you have the faith to believe it, it was also yours.

Well, how does this relate to the subject of abuse? Notice the Bible says "with His wounds we are healed." I'm in the last part of Isaiah 53:5. "The chastisement that brought us peace,"—the kind of sacrifice that was needed to bring us peace—that was upon Him, and with His stripes we are healed. Some people think this means we can have physical healing whenever we want it. Physical healing was included, but we won't get all the blessings until the day of resurrection when we are finally healed.

There's a healing from sin which is paramount in the Psalms as well as in Isaiah—the healing of the soul. That also will never be completed until we are with Jesus. But we begin the journey here, and that's what I am interested in mentioning to you.

Looking at this particular passage of Scripture, we ask ourselves of its relevance. First of all, remember this: Jesus bore what you and I can't bear. I can't bear my sin, iniquities, and my shame. I can't do that. If I were to do that, I'd suffer in hell forever and the process would never end, and you can't do it either. So, Jesus comes along as a Savior and He bears what we can't—our sorrows—and in Hebrews 12:2 it also says that He bore our shame. It says He scorned [despised] shame. I love that phrase. Jesus said to shame, "Shame, shame on you." Jesus bore our shame so we could go free and so that we no longer have to be captivated by it in the shadows.

Listen carefully: An abuser wants to share his shame, he wants to give you his shame. So, you're brought up in an alcoholic home and you bear the shame of your father, and the shame of your relationships, and all of that, that are passed on to you. Listen, you're not Jesus. You're not Jesus. Don't take upon your shoulders the shame of someone else. Jesus is the Savior, and you let Him bear people's shame—but you don't, because shame will hold you bound, shame will keep you in the shadows, and shame will shackle you. And the shame you feel going for help, and the fear you have of your abuser if you go for help has to be cast aside. Here at The Moody Church, we want an atmosphere where it's okay for people to say, "Look at my past. I am broken, I need healing, and here I am." Come out of your shame because of Jesus.

Rodney Clapp has written this: "Does shame bind us? Jesus was bound. Does shame destroy our reputation? The Bible says he was despised and rejected of men. Does shame reduce us to silence? He is led as a lamb to the slaughter, and as a sheep before his shearers is silent so he opens not his mouth. Does shame expose our apparent weaknesses? 'Oh, he saved others. Himself he cannot save,' the multitudes mocked Jesus. Does shame lead to abandonment? 'My God, my God, why hast thou forsaken me?' Does shame diminish us? He was crucified naked, exposed for gawkers to see." Jesus bore our shame. Don't you take someone else's shame. Just deal with your own and expose it to Jesus.

This past week, I read about a woman in a neighborhood abusing a boy in the neighborhood beginning at the age of three. After sexually abusing him, she would chide him and shame him for the fact that he didn't have his clothes on. That woman is evil, but let me tell you a couple of things. First of all, that boy needs to know that the shame he feels is not his. He does not have to feel that shame. He's bearing the shame of an evil woman.

But someone go find that evil woman. Someone track her down. Go into a hovel. Go where she lives and find her, and tell her she can come to Jesus, too, and have her shame taken away. Somebody tell the people out there—the abusers and the abused—that we have a real Savior for real sinners. [*applause*]

Jesus just didn't die for people who committed nominal sins, you know, the sins of the boys and girls in fine Christian homes. Oh no, no, no. A Savior like that won't do for Chicago. A Savior like that won't do for the abuse in our homes. As [Martin] Luther said, "We have a Savior who comes to save us from damnable iniquities," so that woman, too, can stand at the foot of the cross, and her shame can be taken away because we have a real Savior for real sinners. What we need to do today, folks, is to understand that the shame that binds us has to be cast off. We have to come to the light. All of us have done things of which we have been ashamed—and Jesus shamed shame.

Secondly, His abuse brought about our forgiveness. You see, when it says He was wounded for our transgressions, bruised for our iniquities, it was because of that, that Jesus said, "You can now be forgiven and you can be set free." What wonderful news of the gospel. Reconciled to God, reconciled to others, as far as it is possible (there are some people with whom you cannot reconcile), but [you can also be] reconciled with oneself. You'll notice it says, "The chastisement that brought us peace" was upon Him, so you can make peace with the past, so you can know you can be reconciled to God, and in this large audience today, there are some of you who have never been reconciled to God. You've listened to the gospel over and over again, maybe, but you've never understood that what you need to do is to come to Christ. I am urging you to come to Jesus, by whose stripes we are healed. Our sin is taken away; our souls are restored; the process of recovery begins there in the presence of the cross, and some of you need to receive Christ as Savior. And I really do believe that, in a few moments, you're going to, because the Holy Spirit of God is going to be speaking to you, and already is, and you know who you are, don't you?

As a matter of fact, in a few moments, all of us are going to have the opportunity of praying with others, and I'll be explaining that in a moment. But right now, I want you to let the Holy Spirit of God speak to you, and to know we have an abused Savior for abused people. He was raised from the dead, triumphant, and He has borne our iniquities, our sorrows, and He heals our souls' diseases.

> "Bearing shame and scoffing rude,
> In my place condemned He stood,
> Sealed my pardon with His blood:
> Hallelujah, what a Savior!"

Finally, it is because of this reconciliation that having been forgiven, having our shame washed away, we can now, in turn, forgive others. It's necessary to be healed, folks. Whether you are one who's been abused or you're an abuser, forgiveness is necessary.

Someone gave me this story.

In a seminary classroom, a professor, whom we will call Brother Smith, was known for his elaborate object lessons. This day was no exception. On the wall he placed a big target and on a nearby table were many darts (arrows). Brother Smith told the students to draw a picture of someone they disliked or someone they actually hated. Then he would allow them to throw darts at the person's picture. One lady drew a picture of a girl who had stolen her boyfriend. Another drew a picture of a man who had mistreated her. Several drew pictures of those who had abused them. All of the students found someone they hated, and they did so very quickly. For some, the challenge was to limit it to one among so many.

The class lined up and began throwing darts with much laughter and hilarity. Some of the students threw their darts with such force that their targets were ripping apart. Just then Brother Smith interrupted the students and removed the target from the wall. Underneath the target was a picture of Jesus. A hush fell over the room as each student viewed the mangled picture of Jesus. Holes and jagged marks covered His face. His eyes were pierced out. Brother Smith said simply, "Inasmuch as you have done it to the least of these, my brethren, you've done it to me." No other words were necessary as tears filled the eyes of his students. They could not take their eyes off the mangled picture of Jesus. Even after the bell rang, they sat in their seats until one slowly left, and then another, and then another.

My friend, every abuse you ever hurled, whether it's verbal, physical, or sexual, you're hurting Jesus. You mistreat your wife, you are hurting Jesus. You can sling those arrows. You can take [and throw] those darts, but it's Jesus whom you are hurting, and it is the same Jesus who invites the abuser and the abused to come, and says, "Let me take your shame away, let me take your sin away. Let's shine light on this situation so there can be healing." See, that's why we do sing (don't we?) "Hallelujah, what a Savior."

Would you pray now with me please?

Our Father, I ask in the name of Jesus that you might grant to your people the freedom to seek out prayer, and that we all might humble ourselves and know that we need the prayer of others. We acknowledge that we need you. For those who've never trusted Christ, may they do that. In Jesus' name we pray, Amen.

STUDY GUIDE

OBJECTIVE

Marriage, the union of two imperfect individuals, aims to glorify God. This series explores common marital challenges, emphasizing how God's Word guides us to better love our spouses and honor God in our marriages.

moodymedia.org/marriagepuzzle

Watch or listen to Pastor Lutzer's entire sermon series.

ERWIN W. LUTZER

SERMON ONE
RED FLAGS YOU PROBABLY MISSED

THEME
We glorify God in marriage when we seek Him and love our spouse like Christ loves the church.

QUESTIONS
1. In what areas of your marriage are you and your spouse going your own ways, and in what areas can you choose togetherness? How might this choice bring glory to God?

2. How can God use you in your marriage to bless your spouse? In what areas do you struggle to be a blessing? How does blessing your partner glorify God?

3. Since we are all sinners, we all have red flags our partner chooses to ignore. What concerning patterns in your life did your partner choose to overlook? How do you feel knowing they love you despite these?

4. How does the forgiveness a spouse has for their partner reflect God's continual forgiveness of us?

5. Pastor Lutzer noted that only God can bring about lasting change, not any attempt by you. Is this a difficult concept for you to accept? What would entrusting your spouse to God look like in this regard? How might you turn your focus toward your own repentance to better love your spouse as God commands?

6. How often do you try to understand and have sympathy for your spouse? Ask your spouse if they feel understood by you. What steps can you take to grow in sympathy for your spouse?

7. Jesus Christ is our example of how we are to live as children of God. Think through Jesus' ministry and how He responded to those who harmed and belittled Him. Why did He react the way He did, and what does this say about how you are to treat your spouse?

FURTHER READING

Ephesians 5:22–33: How you treat your spouse should not be dependent on how they treat you.

Romans 3:23: Everyone is a sinner before God therefore, you and your spouse both have red flags.

Ephesians 4:32 and Matthew 18:21–35: The Bible clearly instructs believers to forgive each other.

PRAYER FOCUS

Pray that God will give you discernment to see the areas where you are withholding love and grace from your spouse. Despite your spouse's red flags, pray also for God to give you the grace to love them well for His glory. Pray that your marriage may glorify God.

SERMON TWO
MOVING BEYOND YOUR PAST

THEME

We glorify God in our marriages when we accept His forgiveness of our past and forgive our spouse of theirs.

QUESTIONS

1. Pastor Lutzer emphasized the importance of acknowledging your past, confessing your sin, and accepting God's forgiveness. Is there anything for which you need to seek forgiveness and confess to your spouse?

2. When your spouse confesses something to you, how do you respond? Considering what Christ did for you, how should you respond?

3. God forgives as far as the east is from the west (Psalm 103:12). According to Psalm 103:2–9, how does God treat us in light of these forgiven sins?

4. How are you to treat your spouse when you forgive them? As children of God, what should our forgiveness entail?

5. Since the wrath of God is satisfied for you by faith in Christ's work, how does that truth ground how you and your spouse discuss your past?

6. How do you respond when your spouse brings their past sin to you? Does your response acknowledge the sufficiency of Christ's sacrifice for sin?

7. Pastor Lutzer describes how God recycles our pasts for His glory. Consider his example of Solomon, who was born from a marriage that should not have happened, yet he was loved by God. How should knowing this affect your perspective of your past sinfulness and your spouse's?

FURTHER READING
1 Corinthians 6:9–11: Regardless of our past, we were made holy because of Christ.
Romans 8:1, 14–17: We are not defined by what we once were; there is freedom from condemnation for the children of God.

PRAYER FOCUS
Pray that you may be rooted in God's love and accept that you have been forgiven a great debt. Pray that you may love your spouse and forgive them the way you have been loved and forgiven by God. Pray against any record of wrongs you carry against your spouse. Pray that your marriage may glorify God.

SERMON THREE
THE PUZZLE OF YOUR ROLES

THEME

Men and women have allowed culture to influence our understanding of masculinity and femininity. We need guidance from God's Word to understand how spouses should relate to each other in marriage.

QUESTIONS

1. Feminism and pornography have contributed to our unwillingness to commit to traditional roles in marriage. What has shaped your definition of a man and woman and their roles within marriage?

2. Do you agree with John Piper's definition of mature masculinity quoted in this sermon? How would you define mature masculinity? What does the Bible say?

3. John Piper's definition of mature femininity is also quoted. Do you agree with it? How would you define mature femininity? What does the Bible say?

4. Pastor Lutzer points out that the groundwork for marital roles was laid in Genesis' creation narrative. Adam was made first and was tasked to care for the garden before Eve was created. What implications does he draw from this? What does the rest of the creation narrative suggest?

5. As Pastor Lutzer notes, the Hebrew word used for Eve as a "helper" is also used of God. How does this observation shape a Christian view of mature femininity?

6. What does it mean to leave and cleave (Mark 10:7)? Why do you think this is said of the husband? How might a failure to do this harm a marriage?

7. What does Pastor Lutzer say is the ultimate purpose of marriage? What does this mean for husbands? What does it mean for wives?

FURTHER READING
Ephesians 5:22–32: The purpose of marriage is to illustrate the relationship between Christ and the church.
Genesis 1:26–27: God created humankind in His image, giving all of us inherent dignity so that both men and women uniquely reflect God's image.
1 Timothy 2:12–15: God has set apart women for essential roles. Paul links the reason for women's specific role in the church to the creation account.

PRAYER FOCUS
Pray that God will open your heart to His Word, giving you discernment about what's shaped your understanding of the roles of men and women. As you reflect on Ephesians 5, pray for a heart that is willing to submit to Scripture in faith so that you may love your spouse regardless of how they treat you. Pray that your marriage may glorify God.

SERMON FOUR
THE PUZZLE OF THE WILL OF GOD

THEME

Explore God's will for believers, how to discern it, and the possibility of redemption after mistakes, using seven guiding principles.

QUESTIONS

1. James 1:5 exhorts us to ask for wisdom if we lack it. How quick are you to ask for wisdom when you are not sure what you should do? What can you do to grow in this habit?

2. Pastor Lutzer says God loves to guide and lead us. Where have you seen God's guidance in your life? How do you know?

3. Pastor Lutzer suggests that we need to know God's character in order to trust in His will. Why does God's revealed character help us trust in Him and accept His will for us?

4. What does Pastor Lutzer mean when he says the will of God is about *being* rather than *doing*? What do you think about this? What does this mean for us when we face life decisions like those related to vocation, education, etc.?

5. In what ways does living in sin and with a lack of repentance affect our ability to hear and understand God's will?

6. Pastor Lutzer says, "The will of God supersedes our personal happiness." What's your initial response to this statement? How does Christ's request in the garden define this statement (Luke 22:42)?

7. Which of the seven principles was most difficult for you to hear? Why do you think that is?

FURTHER READING
Mark 3:35; John 14:15: Jesus counts those who do God's will as belonging in His family.
Philippians 2:12–13: Because God leads and guides us, we join with God in His work as He works in and through us.
James 4:13–17: Our plans and decisions about the future mustn't be driven by our passions or arrogance but instead by humbly seeking God's will.

PRAYER FOCUS
Pray that God will continue to draw you to Himself, so that you might seek Him more and more. Reflecting on the decisions you have made throughout your life, pray that God would bless the good and wise decisions and redeem the foolish and poor decisions. Pray that your marriage may glorify God.

SERMON FIVE
THE PUZZLE OF YOUR NEEDS AND CONFLICTS

THEME
Marriage presents opportunities for conflict and sin, but also opportunities to love and worship God through devotion to your spouse.

QUESTIONS
1. Conflict is a part of marriage. How do you and your spouse handle marital conflict? How can you both improve how you resolve conflict, keeping in mind your equal worth in God's eyes?

2. Pastor Lutzer cites a book that states a husband's primary need in marriage is to be respected, and a wife's primary need is to be loved. Do you agree with this? Have you seen evidence of this in your marriage?

3. Wives are to submit to their husbands (Ephesians 5:22). What does Pastor Lutzer say submission means? What does it not mean? What should be the basis of a wife's submission to her husband?

4. Husbands are to love their wives (Ephesians 5:25). What does love mean? What does it not mean? What should be the source of our love? Who is our example?

5. According to Pastor Lutzer, what is the purpose of marriage? How can this purpose motivate you to seek to love your spouse better?

6. How are you to act toward your spouse or anyone when you are sinned against? What would Christ do in this situation? What is expected of you as a believer?

7. Husbands are to love their wives as Christ loved the church and gave Himself up for her. Wives are to submit to their husbands as to the Lord. Are there ever any exceptions to these commands according to the Scripture? How are you to treat your spouse when they fail to treat you as they should?

FURTHER READING
1 Peter 3:1–7: A wife's submission to her husband is rooted in her faith in God; the husband's love for his wife is rooted in a desire to keep communion with God unhindered.
Proverbs 19:11: Wisdom guides us to be slow to anger and overlook offenses.
1 Peter 2:23: Jesus did not return sin with sin, but instead committed Himself to God.

PRAYER FOCUS
Pray for God to reveal areas in your marriage where you have not obeyed the biblical command for spouses. Each of you pray for the Lord to give you the strength to care for your spouse as you should. Pray that your faithfulness to the Lord will be evident in your marriage and be for His glory. Pray that your marriage may glorify God.

SERMON SIX
THE PUZZLE OF YOUR FINANCES

THEME

Money promises us happiness and tempts us to place our trust in our bank accounts, but we must trust in God to provide for all our needs.

QUESTIONS

1. What is it about money that touches us so deeply? What does the Bible say about money? How should believers interact with money? How do you interact with money?

2. Why should money be gained honestly? What does it say about someone's faith in God if they use dishonest gains and means? Are you trusting God with your finances?

3. How does contentment bring gain in godliness? What is the danger of being discontent? How content are you with your life at the moment?

4. What does the love of money (greed) lead to? What does the Bible say about the love of money (1 Timothy 6:10)? Would others say that you are greedy?

5. In this sermon, Pastor Lutzer talks about generosity and the importance of putting your wealth in the right place. What did Jesus have to say about moths, rust, and thieves (Matthew 6:19–20)? What are the benefits of being generous? How can you grow in being generous?

6. What does Pastor Lutzer mean when he says, "Lean on God?" How might God use your finances to grow your faith and bring glory to Himself? What can you do to lean on Him more?

7. Do you and your spouse struggle with conflict over money? If not, what have you done to rightly order your wallet? If yes, which of the issues mentioned in this sermon are hardest for you? How can you grow in this?

FURTHER READING
Luke 12:13–20: A man spends his life accumulating wealth, but when he dies, he is not able to take it with him and, therefore, it's worthless to him.
Hebrews 2:10: Everything belongs to God as the Creator of all; therefore, we are not owners but stewards of what we are given.
Acts 20:35: Paul builds on one of the Lord Jesus teachings when He said, "It is more blessed to give than to receive."

PRAYER FOCUS
Pray for the Holy Spirit to convict you of any greed in your (or your spouse's) life. Pray to be delivered from greed and given a heart of generosity to the Lord and others. Pray that your finances will not be a point of tension in your marriage, and that you and your spouse will be united in your desire to use your money as a blessing to God as you steward what He has given you. Pray that your marriage will glorify God.

SERMON SEVEN
THE PUZZLE OF ADDICTIONS

THEME

Pornography, gambling, alcohol…Every addiction promises the world, but delivers heartbreak. We can be delivered from a pattern of shame and fear, and walk in God's light, free from addiction.

QUESTIONS

1. In Proverbs 5:22, we read that the wicked are ensnared by their sin. Have you experienced bondage to sin? Is there an addiction still holding you? How should believers approach God with their habitual sins?

2. What happens when we walk in darkness? How do we have fellowship with God? Why can't we have fellowship with God while we're in darkness?

3. How does addiction feed on fear and shame? What can be done to remove fear and shame? Is there any sin you are hiding from your spouse right now? What do you think the result of that secrecy will be?

4. What are the dangers of self-deception in addiction? What does 1 John 1:5–10 say about our sin? How is God's Word the cure to self-deception?

5. Pastor Lutzer says that one of the things that must be done to walk in the light is to agree with God. How do we agree with God? What does God say about our sin? Are there any sins you are still rationalizing?

6. How does confession release the power of addiction? What should confession lead to? Is there something you need to confess?

7. Take some time apart and pray for the Lord to reveal patterns of sin you need to confess. Come together after prayer and confess to each other and the Lord, then ask for forgiveness. Avoid shaming your spouse, but listen, forgive, and move closer to the Lord together.

FURTHER READING
Luke 8:17: Every hidden sin will be revealed.
1 John 1:9; James 5:16: We are healed through confessing of our sins to God and to one another.
Romans 6:15–23: Believers are no longer slaves to sin, but slaves to righteousness.

PRAYER FOCUS
Pray for the Lord to convict you and your spouse to repent of any remaining sin in your lives. Pray for courage and strength to repent of these sins and confess them to the Lord and each other. Pray for gentleness to not shame your spouse, and for grace to forgive them. To help you overcome temptation, pray for courage to be accountable to both your spouse and others.

SERMON EIGHT
THE PUZZLE OF ABUSE

THEME
Childhood trauma impacts a person's life deeply. Christ's sacrifice heals the believer's shame and restores their dignity as God's children.

QUESTIONS

1. Pastor Lutzer says we are born with a desire to be valued. Where does your value come from? What do you think makes you valuable? What does the Bible have to say about our value?

2. Jesus was rejected and abused and bore the wrath of God for our sin. How are believers healed through His suffering? How have you found comfort in Christ?

3. Our pain can become a burden we were not meant to bear. Is there anything you (or your spouse) need to lay at the feet of Christ? Do the two of you know about each other's pasts? Why is it that, in Christ, we need not be bound by our past?

4. What does it say about God's love that both the abused and the abuser can come to Christ, in faith, and receive His love? What does it say about our value that He can take our shame away? How is God's love different from that of the world?

5. How does Christ's love and forgiveness of us allow us to forgive others? Is there anyone you need to forgive?

6. Think about Pastor Lutzer's story on the dart throwing exercise. What do you think about the "reveal" at the end? Does this change your perspective on your enemies? What should you be motivated to do considering what Christ has suffered on our behalf?

7. Each of you take some time alone to examine your life. Think through any pain that you have experienced, and think about how Christ died bearing the sin of believers to bring us to God. With your spouse, spend time talking about your past sins. Affirm to each other that Christ bore your sins and that you need not feel shame. Spend time worshiping God for giving you value and healing you.

FURTHER READING
1 Peter 2:24: Believers have been healed by Christ's sacrifice.
John 17: Before His betrayal, Christ's concern and prayers are for those who are His.
1 Timothy 1:15: Paul's abuse and persecution of the early churchshows that no one is too sinful and no one's past is too ugly to be beyond God's love and grace.

PRAYER FOCUS
Pray for grace and peace for yourself and your spouse as you reflect on this sermon. Pray that the Holy Spirit would give you the ability to forgive those you need to forgive, and to ask forgiveness of those you have wronged. Pray that you will find dignity and healing in Christ.

THE MARRIAGE PUZZLE

Made in the USA
Monee, IL
16 September 2024

65908725R00085